HENDERSON
ON CORPORATE STRATEGY

HENDERSON
ON CORPORATE STRATEGY

Bruce D. Henderson

Abt Books

Cambridge, Massachusetts

Second printing

Library of Congress Catalog Card Number 78-72889

© The Boston Consulting Group, Inc., 1979

Printed in the United States of America.

ISBN: 0-89011-526-5

This book is dedicated to the working professionals of BCG and their clients who provided all of the stimulation for the concepts and convictions which are expressed herein.

CONTENTS

PREFACE

This book contains selected essays on business written over about ten years. They were derived from ideas stimulated by the professional work of The Boston Consulting Group, Inc.

Because of their original use they were confined in length to no more than about 1500 words. They were written exclusively for an audience of senior management in large scale industrial enterprise. Assumptions about the audience significantly affected style and content. Statements that such an audience would find believable were not supported. Only the provocative material was argued. The subject matter was chosen to be deliberately provocative, significant in implication, and relevant to the policy decisions of corporate competition.

Over the years these essays were mailed by The Boston Consulting Group, Inc. to its clients and potential clients all over the world. A large proportion of them were translated into French, German, Italian and Japanese as well. There seems to be little doubt that the ideas and concepts of business worldwide have been shaped and modified in a significant way by these modest essays.

The "Perspectives" contained in this book are selections from the more than two hundred which have been written and published. The demand for reprints and past copies seems endless. This compendium is a response to that demand.

Bruce Henderson

I

CORPORATE STRATEGY

1

BUSINESS STRATEGY TODAY

Since the beginning of business, all firms have had plans and all firms have followed some kind of strategy. Characteristically, both the plans and the strategy have been intuitive or traditional. However, the increasing pace of change is forcing management to make their strategies explicit and often to change them. Strategy as such is getting more and more attention.

There are many ways of thinking about strategy development. In a static sense it can be thought of in terms of strengths and weaknesses. By using military parallel, it is possible to think of it in terms of concentration of strength against competitors' weaknesses. However, the military analogy has only a limited application to business because business is a continuing process, not just a battle, a campaign, or even a war to be won and finished.

More useful concepts of corporate strategy relate the firm to its competitors in terms of a competitive system in equilibrium. Any really useful strategy must include a means of upsetting the competitive equilibrium and re-establishing it again on a more favorable basis. This is why strategy is more than a posture or a pattern; it is a dynamic concept involving sequence, timing, and competitive reaction.

Mathematics has made a contribution to strategy, particularly in terms of decision theory and risk evaluation. However, there are broad problems of strategy in which the critical factor depends upon perceptions, attitudes, and business brinkmanship. Strategy is far more than an application of logic. In any given business it is usually the reaction or initiative of a few key competitors who determine the stability of the competitive situation. Assessment and use of competitors' behavioral characteristics often require the exercise of business brinkmanship.

Any approach to strategy quickly encounters a conflict between corporate objectives and corporate capabilities. Attempting the impossible is not good strategy; it is just a waste of resources. On the other hand, setting inadequate objectives is obviously self-defeating. However, setting the proper objectives depends upon prejudgment of the potential success of the strategy used. Yet, you cannot determine the strategy until you know the objectives. Strategy development is thus a reiterative process requiring art as well as science.

Some of the frustrations we have just mentioned may account for the fact that many corporate strategies are traditional and intuitive rather than logical and tightly reasoned. But there *are* concepts and techniques which are of great value in approximating the opportunities of a corporation and speeding up the process of strategy development.

One of these concepts, for example, involves market segmentation. This has its military parallel in terms of isolating the battlefield. There are also some parallels with the duelist's choice of weapons, although in business it is the challenger who has the choice.

A market can be viewed in many different ways, and a product can be used in many different ways. Each time the product-market pairing is varied, the relative competitive strength is varied too. Many businessmen do not recognize that a key element in strategy is choosing the competitor whom you wish to challenge, as well as choosing the market segment and product characteristics with which you will compete.

Business has only financial objectives in the final analysis. Judicious use of financial insight can be a major strategic weapon. It is easy to demonstrate that in some industries superior financial policies can be the equivalent of twenty, thirty, forty percent or greater differential in selling price. The financial equivalent of that price/cost differential can permit price reductions of that magnitude and still achieve the same results in profit, growth, and return to stockholders with the same underlying cost structure. Strategic use of this kind of potential differential is heavily dependent on effective risk analysis and on accurate determination of the true cost of capital. To be effective, this approach to strategy must be based on system analysis, not factor evaluation.

It is interesting to observe that many companies make intuitive decisions which are often correct, even though they are in direct contradiction to the logic of the policies they state. This reflects the highly intuitive character of such policies. For example, many companies state that they will not undertake any investments in which the before tax return on assets is less than, say, twenty percent. Yet, they will make investments in certain kinds of projects with far less return than this. Company consumer finance operations are a typical example. This paradox has a sound basis even though it is unstated. But it need not be so implicit. There are ways of equating risk, return, and cost of capital. These relations can be used in such a way that competitive advantages will, in fact, be optimized.

Over the past several years the fast pace of some industries, such as electronics, aerospace, and certain kinds of chemicals, has dramatized the need for industrial economic concepts. It is now beginning to appear that technology and economics can be related in a quantitative fashion in a dynamic model. It is possible to approximate the effect of interaction between competitors when technical progress is a major factor. For example, it now seems practical to place an approximate price tag on the value of a change in market share and evaluate the return on investment, even for a fast-moving, rapidly growing technical product.

Many of these newer concepts produce real problems of internal organization. In a dynamic economy, all of the factors of technology, finance, marketing, and competitive economics are interrelated. Optimizing functions instead of the whole company is far from adequate to produce superior corporate performance. Such organizational concepts leave only the chief executive in a position to think in terms of the corporation as a whole.

Complex corporations have tried in many ways to broaden the scope of the chief executive in dealing with such complexities. Many of these approaches were well suited to a slower paced economy and nonintegrated operations. The profit center concept was one such approach.

Unfortunately, the profit center concept emphasizes short-term consequences, which are often transient, rather than shifts in competitive equilibrium over time. Even worse, it is disfunctional when it optimizes the profit center instead of the corporation as a whole.

Innovations in organization have also become necessary. The computer has provided some assistance, and specialized staff has been useful in many cases. However, it is becoming increasingly necessary to find a more effective organizational arrangement for dealing with corporate strategy on a continuing basis. Many companies do need to relate separate businesses. Each business may be facing major policy choices which are of far-reaching significance to the future of each such business. Yet each business must be related to the company as a whole and its objectives too.

The accelerating rate of change is producing a business world in which customary managerial habits and organization are increasingly inadequate. Experience was an adequate guide when changes could be made in small increments. But intuitive and experience-based management philosophies are grossly inadequate when decisions are strategic and have major irreversible consequences. Supersonic airliners, antimissile missile systems, and a common computer language, for example, are producing such obvious problems that the management alternatives are being discussed in the public press. Fortunately, the state of the art in strategy development is itself changing at an accelerating rate.

Strategy concepts need to be explicit in order to be executed in a coordinated fashion in complex organizations. But concepts are the very thing that have been missing from strategy discussions in businesses in the past. Now, more than ever before, the rewards for a conceptual model of the business appear to be pyramiding. Those managers who can conceptualize their strategy and make it explicit in terms of a system of competition will dominate their businesses in the future.

There are an increasing number of conceptual models of business relationships. Many of these can be quantified enough to at least establish the sensitivity of the various factors and to determine the stability or instability of the various relationships.

The fact that these concepts can be quantified also means that they can be programmed for a computer. This now offers the opportunity for economically and quickly exploring a range of combinations and alternatives that was utterly impossible a short while ago. Perhaps more important, this machine-man interface is vastly accelerating the learning process by which a manager acquires a complete grasp of complex relationships. The combination of new concepts plus new techniques promises a major acceleration in the development of explicit strategies.

Strategy development for business is only in its infancy. It is still very much an intuitive art, although both concepts and techniques are available to change this art into something closer to a logical, explicit, and orderly analysis. Strategy is something quite different from administrative skills. Unfortunately, the two are typically grouped together under the heading of "Management."

One prediction seems safe: explicit and sophisticated approaches to strategy are emerging. The rewards for developing a superior business strategy are great. The state of the art can be expected to move extremely fast in the immediate future.

THE STRATEGIC PERSPECTIVE:
Growth and Equilibrium

In most firms strategy tends to be intuitive and based upon traditional patterns of behavior which have been successful in the past. In growth industries or in a changing environment, this kind of strategy is rarely adequate. In any company a significant improvement in performance over time usually depends upon a change in strategy if previous operations have been competently managed.

A significant change in strategy is always a momentous and difficult process. It requires a complete rethinking of the organization's objectives, resources, and competitive relationships. The change itself requires a reorientation of values at every level in the organization if the change is to be implemented effectively. Good corporate strategy needs to be explicitly stated and the objectives need to be widely understood even if the underlying reasoning is not revealed.

When the growth rate exceeds the cost of capital, the competitive relationships become inherently unstable. Aggressive competition then produces revolution instead of evolution in competitive relationships.

A growth situation is fundamentally different, in its strategy requirements, from a normal competitive relationship. All large businesses were once small. At some time in their growth they passed through a high growth rate period. What made for success then is not necessarily appropriate later.

A business should be regarded as a system in equilibrium. An effective corporate strategy is a predetermined sequence for the allocation of resources in such a fashion that the equilibrium will be shifted to a more favorable relationship.

To examine equilibrium in this sense requires system analysis of financial, technoeconomic, brinkmanship, and organizational factors, in addition to the effects of accelerated growth rate.

Financial Strategies

Astute use of financial resources can often produce competitive advantages equal to many years of normal growth. It is easy to demonstrate that in some industries financial policies can produce the equivalent of a ten, twenty, thirty percent or more differential in costs relative to otherwise equivalent competitors.

There is a convincing amount of evidence that in growth industries this particular kind of financial leverage can be reconverted directly into an essentially permanent differential in product cost, as well as a differential in market participation.

Failure to use corporate assets aggressively not only makes a company vulnerable in its markets but, equally important, can cause the company to be raided, the purchase funded in fact with the company's own money.

Aside from financial strategies of competition, there are often major opportunities for achieving corporate goals through financial engineering. When market, tax, or book values are not congruent, there is usually an opportunity to arbitrate the difference and convert it into a strategic advantage.

Market Strategies

Market strategies are all based upon segmentation and concentration of resources. A market can be viewed in many different ways, and each time the market-product pairing is varied, the relative competitive capability is changed also.

Segmentation implicitly means identifiying competitors, and their resources relative to yours, for each relevant market-product pairing. Successful market strategies in effect segment the total market in a way that minimizes competitors' strengths while maximizing yours. The parallel in military strategy is "isolating the battlefield." Control Data's spectacular success in entering the computer market against IBM is a classic example of astute segmentation. Most dramatically successful business strategies are based on market segmentation and concentration of resources in that segment.

Technoeconomic Product Strategies

There is an impressive array of evidence that cost, price, margin, market share, and accumulated experience are directly related in a characteristic pattern. This pattern can be used in a predictive fashion to see what would normally be expected to happen if individual competitors chose various alternatives in their own strategy. These consequences involve the combined effects of technology, scale, organizational effectiveness, financial constraints, and market elasticity.

It is possible to demonstrate that, at various stages of product development, the critical strategy element shifts from technical lead, to financial resources, to organizational policy coordination, and finally to market share.

It is also possible to demonstrate that competitive equilibrium is highly unstable under certain conditions, conditionally unstable under others, and finally the equilibrium is almost certain to become essentially stable.

Brinkmanship Strategies

It is not usually recognized that competitive equilibrium must be the result of voluntary self-restraint by all competitors. If this were not true, then unlimited competition would exhaust the resources of successive competitors until only one survived. This does not happen because individual competitors become convinced that their best interests are served by not pushing competition beyond a certain point. Sometimes this point is determined by the lack of incremental reward, even if the competition is successful. More commonly, self-restraint is imposed by expectations about competitive reactions.

It follows that appraisal of probable competitive reaction is critical to predicting the consequences of any strategy. It also follows that anything which influences competitive decision making can be of great importance. All improvements in market share, for example, depend upon convincing competitors that it will not be worthwhile to invest in serving a larger market.

Business brinkmanship is based on the recognition that (1) competition has a psychological and emotional side; (2) it is absolutely necessary to understand the irrational content and emotional biases of competitors' behavior; and (3) indeed, success in business is often linked with the ability to predict and capitalize on the response of competitors to your strategic actions.

Strategy and Organization

Different kinds of organization are required to implement different kinds of strategy. There must be tradeoffs between degree of coordination, speed of response, dependability of behavior, and amount and kind of information available. The vast difference between military organization and that of a university derives from more than tradition and cultural background. The differences reflect very real requirements for effective specialization of decision making in dissimilar environments requiring dissimilar deployment and control of resources.

For the corporation with multiple products and multiple profit centers or administrative units, organizational form automatically limits potential strategies.

Business Strategy on an International Scale

Competition across national boundaries is becoming increasingly significant. This is both a major opportunity and a major added threat. In effect, the business chess game becomes three-dimensional. This added dimension has its own special characteristics. Unless these are understood in terms of long-term equilibrium, they can provide very unpleasant surprises.

The producer with the largest home market has some significant strategic advantages if other things are equal. Capitalizing on this advantage usually requires quite different strategies, however, from those which were successful in that home market.

THE FUNDAMENTAL RULE OF STRATEGY

"Induce your competitors not to invest in those products, markets, and services where you expect to invest the most." That is the fundamental rule of strategy.

Competitors determine your market share. Competitors determine your price. Competitors determine your return on investment. They do this by their investments.

If your competitors invest much more rapidly than the market grows, there is almost no way for anyone to make a profit. If competitors for any reason avoid investment in a given business, then there is no real limit on the market share or price level of those who are willing to invest in advance to supply the market.

After periods of inflation, it is usually unnecessary to dissuade competitors from investing. This is particularly true if inflation has been followed by depression. Inflation is always followed by "stagflation" before prosperity returns. In periods such as 1976, competitors do not invest. They have been persuaded. The problem changes to convincing yourself to invest in the face of apparently far from adequate returns.

Inflation makes the return on new investment seem correspondingly low compared to the return on capacity bought at pre-inflation prices.

Inflation makes the required minimum return higher by the amount of inflation itself just to finance the inflation.

The recession following inflation makes the need for added capacity seem distant.

The liquidity squeeze that ends inflation makes new debt to both finance inflation and add capacity seem like double jeopardy.

Inflation persuades all, or nearly all, competitors to underinvest.

Yet failure to invest at a rate equal to physical market growth plus inflation plus depreciation will inevitably lead to shortages. Shortages lead to higher prices. Prices must inevitably rise until the apparent return induces enough investment to relieve the shortage. It must be this way sooner or later.

Those who have additional existing capacity during a period of shortage and extended delivery are inevitably able to achieve a market share equivalent to their then available capacity.

If an increase in market share is achieved, it can and should result in a proportionate reduction in cost due to the experience curve effect. Increased market share times increased cost differential leads to an exponential increase in profit multiplied by the added margin required to induce others also to invest in added capacity. Thus, for those with the foresight, resources, and wisdom to invest in capacity before others are willing to do so, the rewards can be high.

The obvious risk-free place to invest is in those product-market areas where you are already the leader and low-cost competitor. The risk must be less for you than for those who have higher costs. The profitable company is rare indeed which does not make most of its profit in those few product-market sectors in which it is the acknowledged leader or very close to being the leader.

Those products and markets where someone else is the clear-cut leader are impregnable if the leader has achieved his cost potential, is well managed, and well financed. However, such leaders are often overtaken and passed by higher cost competitors when such leaders optimize short-term performance instead of long-term competitive advantage.

If you have the will and the resources to invest, then periods following high inflation, recession, and liqudity squeeze are periods of major opportunity. These are the periods in which it is not necessary to discourage investment by competitors — they have already been discouraged.

Unless you believe that inflation is permanently over and will not need to be financed, unless you believe that industry growth has stopped and no more capacity will be needed, unless you believe that prices will never rise enough to justify further investment, then it should be obvious that investing in capacity before it is needed will be handsomely rewarded. You will be severely punished if you wait to invest until you are already out of capacity while your competitors did not wait.

However it is done and whatever the business climate, the fundamental rule of strategy remains the same. You must directly or indirectly induce your competitors to refrain from investment in those areas which you find the most attractive for investment. It has been done many times before. If it had not, you would not see high-cost, low-share challengers take away the market share of entrenched, low-cost leaders.

BUSINESS STRATEGY CONCEPTS

Spectacular business successes are usually new ways of doing business in familiar markets with familiar products. These are the true strategic victories, won by using corporate resources to substantially outperform a competitor with superior strength.

The concept of superior performance without superior resources is usually identified with trying harder. Yet most companies seem to work very hard to produce only minor differentials in performance.

The underlying principle of a good strategy is simple: "Concentrate your strength against your competitor's relative weakness." This principle has a major corollary in a dynamic competitive environment: concentration of effort will inevitably produce a counter-concentration by competition; therefore, timing and sequence are critical. A major attack should never be launched against a competent, well-entrenched competitor without first eliminating his ability or willingness to respond in kind.

There are many prerequisites to a successful strategy:

The characteristics of the competition must be known in detail, including characteristic attitudes and behavior.

The environment in which competition will take place must be equally well understood.

Your own relative strengths must be accurately and objectively appraised.

The strategic concept must not be based on the obvious exercise of known strengths. If it is, you don't need a strategy, just a plan.

It must be possible to achieve stability if the strategy succeeds.

Your own organization must not be misled by your efforts to outmaneuver competition. Strategic goals must be very explicit.

Once the strategic framework has been designed, the tactics of attack must be selected. Concentration of resources can be achieved in several ways:

Choose the most vulnerable market segment.

Choose products or markets which require response rates beyond a competitor's ability.

Choose products or markets which require capital that a competitor is unwilling to commit.

Recognize the commercial potential of new technology early.

Exploit managerial differences in style, method, or system, such as overhead rate, distribution channels, market image, or flexibility.

The value of the initiative depends on when and how the competition responds. Therefore, an effective strategy must choose the best initiative and also dissuade competition from responding. This is a fundamental strategic concept that is often neglected. Strategic success almost always depends upon the competitor's decision not to compete. Therefore, ability to influence the competitor's decision is critical. It is necessary to win in the mind of the competition.

Diversion and dissuasion fall into classic categories:

Appear to be unworthy of attention. Quickly cut off a part of the market which is too small to justify a major response. Repeat.

Appear to be unbeatable. Convince competitors that if they follow your lead and practices, they will gain nothing since you will equal or better any market actions they take.

Avoid attention. Be secretive. Do not let competitors know about new products, policies, or capabilities until it is too late for them to respond effectively.

Redirect attention. Focus competitive attention on the major volume areas of company sales, not on the high-potential areas.

Attract attention but discredit significance. Overstate and overpublicize the potentials of new products or policies.

Appear to be irrational. Take actions which seem emotional or implusive but which make competitive investment unattractive.

These and other patterns have exact counterparts in military behavior. In business as in war, the lessons of experience teach the same thing:

. . . We can at least crystallize the lessons into two simple maxims — one negative, the other positive. The first is that, in the face of the overwhelming evidence of history, no general is justified in launching his troops in a direct attack upon an enemy firmly in position. The second, that instead of seeking to upset the enemy's equilibrium by one's attack, it must be upset before a real attack is, or can be, successfully launched.[1]

Liddell Hart, Strategy

A GUIDELINE FOR BUSINESS STRATEGY

Any businessman who can answer certain basic questions better than his competitors has a major strategic advantage. Most of these questions are asked constantly, in one form or another, in virtually every company:

What are my competitors's costs?

Why do I make money on one product but lose money on an equally good one?

How shall I price this new product?

How much is more market share worth for a given product? Alternatively, what are *all* the costs of losing market share?

Should I lower prices? When? By how much?

How much capacity shall I add? When?

What will prices be next year? Five years from now?

Why have my prices broken so sharply? When will the decline stop?

All these issues are part of a single fundamental question: why does one competitor outperform another (assuming comparable management skills and resources)? Are there basic rules for success?

There do indeed appear to be rules for success, and they relate to the impact of accumulated experience on competitors' costs, industry prices, and the interrelations between the two.

Prices

It is a matter of nearly everyone's experience that the price of a new product declines after its initial introduction and as the product becomes more widely produced and commonly available.

In recent years, the rate of new product growth in some markets has been so high that it has been easy to observe the price decline during the early life of many new products. With some, such as semiconductor devices, the postintroduction decline has been so rapid that it has been the subject of considerable attention in the industry.

It is not commonly recognized that price declines follow a remarkably consistent pattern and that the pattern appears to apply to a wide range of products. The characteristic pattern is one in which the price declines by a constant percentage with each doubling of the total number of units produced by the entire industry.

This kind of decline has previously been observed in the labor cost element of various products. In describing the decline in the hours of labor required to produce a product, it has become customary to speak of a "learning curve." Hirschmann[1] recently reviewed many aspects of the learning curve and pointed out its importance as a tool of operating management. Texas Instruments Corporation[2] has used its knowledge of this relationship in the semiconductors market to set management objectives.

Costs

If prices decline according to a set pattern, then *costs* of successful producers must behave in a similar manner. Costs declining more slowly would eventually exceed prices. Costs declining more rapidly, by steadily increasing profits, would attract more competition and capacity, with a resulting pressure for price declines.

The key phenomenon, then, is the decline of unit cost made possible by increased experience, even though most (but not all) of our observed data relate the decline of *unit price* to increased experience.

There is a natural reluctance to accept the possibility that costs can always be reduced. Although Hirschmann's paper argues this point effectively, it is worth emphasizing the reasons for its

---

[1] Winfred B. Hirschmann, "Profit From the Learning Curve," *Harvard Business Review*, January-February 1964, pp. 125-139.

[2] "Texas Instruments: All Systems Go," *Duns Review*, January 1967, p. 25 et seq.

plausibility. For example, we are accustomed to an annual and substantial increase in national manufacturing productivity measured in terms of real output per man-hour. Why should this occur year after year?

Some of the improvements may be due to the fact that operatives have learned to perform their production tasks more effectively. Some of the improvement may be caused by the adoption of better methods, scheduling, and work organization. Some may be ascribed to improved tools and capital investments. Even so, a major cause of increases in productivity is technological change, which periodically provides a new basis to which the traditional improvements can be applied.

Implications for Business Strategy

The implications of such cost behavior are profound indeed. The concepts of competition, return on investment, public policy, and corporate strategy are all affected.

The most important implication, by far, is that competitive relationships are not stable. If gains in market share (and thus accumulated experience) produce lower costs *relative to competition,* then this can be converted into further increases in market share. This, of course, suggests a significant influence on corporate strategy potentials.

If costs, prices, volume, and relative earning power over time can be quantitatively related to each other, then we have a powerful tool for evaluating strategy alternatives. This, in fact, seems to be the potential which cost/volume and price/volume slopes offer and is a compelling reason to understand the characteristic behavior thoroughly.

In a sense, this insight is not basically different from the well-known learning curve phenomenon. However, the implications are far more profound than the mere prediction of labor costs. It appears that the basic relationship applies to the full range of costs, including development, capital, distribution, and overhead, as well as labor costs. Furthermore, the characteristic relationships among competitors seem to be determined by these patterns.

If this concept is valid, then we can predict the conditions under which relationships among competitors will stabilize.

CONSTRUCTION OF A BUSINESS STRATEGY

Most companies feel they are in a highly competitive business. Most companies regard their competitors as the principal obstacle to either higher profits or faster growth. This is natural and proper. The question is how to compete.

Strategy is the manner of using resources which is expected to provide superior results in spite of a competitor's otherwise equal or superior capabilities.

Games have been classified as: (1) games of chance, (2) games of skill, and (3) games of strategy. For the purpose of this discussion, assume that chance and skill are equally distributed. How can a business firm develop a superior strategy?

We can assume that each firm is relatively free to choose its businesses. This choice can be expressed in terms of product line, market segments, geographical coverage, or other elements. However, the choice of business also determines the competition. Therefore, freedom to choose the business means freedom to choose who the competitors will be.

Firms are never identical. They have different histories and traditions, different resources, different reputations, different management styles, and often different objectives. These differences may be either strengths or weaknesses, depending upon the strategy chosen. We can assume that such differences exist, and that they are important to the choice of strategy.

We can also assume that neither your own nor your competitor's objectives are simple or obvious. There are many tradeoffs between near-term and long-term profits; growth and profits; growth in assets and growth in reported profits; stability and growth; dividends and growth; and stockholders, employees, creditors, and others. It is reasonable to assume that these differences will result in different goals for different competitors.

It is also safe to assume that the future will produce a substantial amount of change in technology, markets, and competitors. Any strategy must take this change into account.

Based upon these assumptions, the starting point for strategy development should be:

1. definition of the business area involved
2. identification of the significant competitors in that business area

3. identification of the differences between you and the significant competitors
4. forecast of the changes in the environment which can affect the competition
5. identification of your own objectives and any known differences between them and those of competitors

These are all obvious factors, but they should be made explicit since a change in one requires a re-examination of the entire sequence.

The difficult part of constructing a strategy is the development of the strategy concept. Any strategy of value requires that you follow a different course from your competitors; or initiate action which will not be effective for the competitor if he attempts to emulate you; or follow a course which will have quite different, and more favorable, consequences for you than for your competitor.

The essential element of successful strategy is that it derives its success from the differences between competitors, with a consequent difference in their behavior. Ordinarily, this means that any corporate policy and plan which is typical of the industry is doomed to mediocrity. Where this is not so, it should be possible to demonstrate that all *other* competitors are at a distinct disadvantage.

Strategy development, then, consists of conceiving of ways and means to emphasize the value of the differences between you and your competitors. The normal procedure includes the following sequence:

1. Start with the present business as it now is.
2. Forecast what will happen to its environment in general over a reasonable period of years. This includes markets, technology, industry volume, and competitive behavior.
3. Predict what your performance will be over this period if you continue with no significant change in your policies or methods of operation.
4. If this is fully satisfactory, then stop there, since you do not need to develop any further to achieve satisfaction. If the prediction is not fully satisfying, then continue.
5. Appraise the significant strengths and weaknesses that you have in comparison to your more important competitors. This appraisal should include any factors which may become important (finance, marketing ability, technology, costs, organization, morale, reputation, management depth, etc.).

6. Evaluate the differences between your policies and strategies and those of your major competitors.

7. Attempt to conceive of some variation in policy or strategy which would improve your competitive posture in the future.

8. Appraise the proposed alternate strategy in terms of possible risks, competitive response, and potential payout. Evaluate in terms of minimum acceptable corporate performance.

9. If this is satisfactory, then stop strategy development and concentrate on planning the implementation.

10. If a satisfactory result has not been found in the previous stages, then broaden the definition of the present business and repeat the cycle above. Ordinarily, redefinition of the business means looking at other products you can supply to a market which you know and understand. Sometimes it means supplying existing products to a different market. Less frequently, it means applying technical or financial abilities to new products and new markets simultaneously.

11. The process of broadening the definition of the business to provide a wide horizon can be continued until one of the following occurs:
    a. The knowledge of the new area becomes so thin that a choice of the sector to study becomes intuitive or based upon obviously inadequate judgment.
    b. The cost of studying the new area becomes prohibitively expensive because of lack of related experience.
    c. It becomes clear that the prospects of finding a competitive opportunity are remote.

12. If the existing business is not satisfactory and no attempt to broaden it offers satisfactory prospects, then only two alternatives exist:
    a. Lower the performance expectations.
    b. Reverse the process and attempt to find an orderly method of disinvestment.

The critical element in strategy development is the development of a concept. This is an inherently intuitive and cut-and-try process, even though first-class staff research is an absolutely essential prerequisite to success.

Thus, the process of constructing a business strategy tends to be a continuous cycle. It cannot be otherwise. Strategy development is an art, not a science.

CORPORATE STYLE AND CORPORATE STRATEGY

Strategy Dynamics

The strategies required for growth are utterly different from those required to maximize profit on a static business. Many of the usual controls and measures of performance are misleading and sometimes dysfunctional.

For static businesses and products, the near-term cash payouts represent a large portion of the present value, even though the profitability may continue forever. By contrast, virtually the entire present value of growth products depends upon volume, profit margin, and cash throwoff after growth has subsided.

This produces an apparent paradox. Static products appear highly profitable but present no investment potential. Growth products offer a very high investment return but depress profits and are not self-financing. Conventional management control measurement obscures the very large strategy opportunity that is implicit in these relationships.

Financial Strategy

All business strategies can be cast in financial terms since return on equity investment is the common denominator. Fundamentally, this is the value of cash put in compared with the value of cash returned later.

The short-term performance measurements can become inverted where there is a dynamic factor in apparent investment return because of growth. Less debt can become more risky than more debt. Lower prices can produce a higher return on investment than higher prices. Many financial measurements which are useful and valid in steady-state or static situations are strategic traps in growth situations.

These financial misperceptions can be converted into very potent competitive strategies. The conventional management controls can prevent competitors from reacting to aggressive strategies or perceiving the missed opportunities.

Experience Cost and Price Policy

Much of the dynamic character of growth products results from the influence of growth on costs. Rate of growth can be directly related to rate of decline in costs by Experience Curve Theory, which states that differences in growth rate will result in progressively greater differences in cost. Characteristically, this cost difference is translated back into continued differences in growth rate. The result, of course, is a continuing shift in relative ability to compete.

Shifts in competitive capability are almost always reflected in either price behavior or shifts in market share penetration. However, different competitors have different attitudes toward price level and growth rate. These differences are fundamental consequences of market and production economies, as well as corporate history. Because this is true, it is possible both to explain and to predict characteristic price behavior. Experience Curve Theory provides a full integration of the relationships among growth, market share, cost, price, and competitive stability. Competitors' attitudes are the only significant unknown variable. Good businessmen should know their competitors.

Computers and Strategy

Successful and experienced businessmen have an intuitive feel for many strategic relationships. Unfortunately even intuitive genius has severe limitations in practice. In the absence of a conceptual base, it is impossible to communicate or teach the basis for decision. Alternatives cannot be explored by discussion or logic. Optimization is impractical because sensitivity cannot be checked. This leads inevitably to strategy conservatism or unacceptable risks in spite of insight and intuitive genius.

However, even when these concepts are made explicit and are well understood, they are still complex in terms of calculation and analysis. Before the advent of computers, many of these relationships were too difficult to calculate in any practical fashion. They were used either intuitively or not at all.

Modern computers provide the necessary means to translate concepts into simulations and models. With computers, many things can be explored which would otherwise be merely a matter of conjecture or opinion. This kind of process underlies the dramatic improvement in inventory utilization in the last decade. However, simulation can be applied to strategy models of the business concepts as easily as it can to inventory models or decision rules.

The really significant application of the computer is in policy formulation. If the concepts and relationships are made explicit, it is possible to use computers to simulate the reaction of the business to policy changes. Only in this way is it possible to optimize the differences in policies over time for the different products that constitute a modern diversified business. A similar process has been used for years to teach captains of jetliners how to adjust to the differences among similar aircraft of great complexity and cost. The rewards for business strategy simulation are far greater than those for jet aircraft flight simulation.

Acquisitions and Strategy

Evaluation of strategy alternatives often points to the need for more change in corporate resource application. Acquisitions are often a useful way to cause an instant recapitalization of the company, an instant increase in debt capacity, or an instant opening of major investment opportunities. Often, acquisitions provide one time instant increases in *reported* earning. Yet, by itself, acquisition can merely convert a mediocre company into a larger, less manageable, equally mediocre company. The real payoffs in acquisitions come from sequential fitting of companies into a strategic plan which requires specific elements at specific times. Acquisitions are a means to an end, not an end in themselves. Evaluation of true synergy is possible only in the context of a strategy concept.

Organization and Strategy

Business optimization has profound implications for business organization as well as for policy formulation. During the fifties, there was a near fad of decentralization and line-staff organization. This was a natural attempt to deal with increasing complexity, size, and diversity by mixing specialization and dispersion of authority.

Yet, present concepts of business dynamics demonstrate dramatically that there are no independent parts of any corporation if it has any reason for being a single corporation. Operations must be decentralized as a practical matter. They are too complex and too diverse. Simultaneously, the choice of objectives, the coordination of action, and the implementation must be conceived, evaluated, optimized, planned, and programmed centrally. The individual units of a corporation are no more independent profit centers than the ships in a navy are independent of each other's behavior.

Management Style and Strategy

The conclusion seems inescapable that the combination of dynamic business concepts, growth potential, and computers requires a basically different management style for competitive success than the traditional approaches of the past. There are multiple examples of companies who grow into giant, diversified corporations from humble beginnings, far outstripping their more traditional competitors. Perhaps they take far greater risks in their growth period, but they seem to more than compensate by their greater relative strength when they succeed. Yet, it takes a concept of the business as an integrated dynamic whole in equilibrium with its competitive environment to be able to evaluate alternate risks versus rewards. That evaluation, of course, is the essence of business policy, investment, and management.

INTUITIVE STRATEGY

Strategy formulation does not come easily even for the experienced executive. The seasoned executive has many years of trial and error behind him in his administrative skills. He has learned from many mistakes; he has been conditioned. He knows what happens if he does something different. None of this applies to strategy.

Strategy cannot be changed very often. It is, by definition, the essentially irretrievable commitment of resources. Consequently, few executives ever see strategy changed. It is almost never possible to know what alternative strategies would have accomplished. In any case, strategy decisions are not visible except to senior executives. Real exposure to strategy considerations does not begin until near the peak of an executive's career.

Neither experience nor intuition is of much help in strategy formulation even if both are vital to implementation. Systematic analysis of competitive equilibrium is the only technique that works. This kind of analysis is not a normal executive skill or requirement. It is also a way of thinking that is difficult to learn.

The multidivision corporation with multiple products and numerous overlapping competitors is a particularly complex strategy problem because it has so many alternatives open. The usual solution is to break the problem down to manageable size by dividing the company into profit centers and treating each as if it were an independent operation.

However, profit centers offer no genuine solution to this complexity. Profit center optimization is certain to be suboptimization for the corporation as a whole. The results are almost sure to fall far short of the company's potential.

Profit centers are not and cannot be independent; they share common financial resources. As a consequence, the actions of one profit center automatically place constraints on the others. Furthermore, each profit center has differing opportunities to use the common resources. The activities of each profit center have quite differing effects on common competitors.

The whole competitive system must be optimized at once in order to improve performance. Competitors, too, are always very much a part of the system, and their reactions must be integrated in the analysis. Strategy and performance can be optimized only if the whole system is fully understood.

Most significant multidivision companies can be more profitable, grow faster, and simultaneously lower prices even if their operating efficiency is unchanged. Corporate performance is a function of corporate strategy and control as a whole, not the sum of individual profit centers or product strategies.

Product portfolio strategy is the real basis for competitive superiority among multidivision, multiproduct companies. All product markets should not be treated alike. Some products should supply investment opportunities; others should supply the funds to invest. Current profitability is not the measure of performance, value, or of appropriate management objectives.

Some products are highly profitable but have no future except
to generate cash. They are not an investment opportunity
now.

Others are very unprofitable now but can be richly rewarding
if the appropriate investment is made soon enough.

Some products are profitable now, but the real payoffs will
come later if position is merely maintained.

Other products appear profitable but in fact will be cash traps
forever.

Choices of this kind are not made well by intuition. Nor are most
companies equipped to make them using a systems approach.

Each product in the multidivision portfolio has a different
role, a different use, and requires a different objective. The use of
identical goals and common objectives for all profit centers is a certain and guaranteed way to insure inferior performance.

The utility of each product in a company's portfolio cannot be
determined except with reference to the product portfolio of the
significant competitors. The match between product portfolios in
business can be as critical as the match between the cards held in a
poker game. In both cases, the proper use of superiority can result
in the winner taking all. In both cases it is perceived relative strength
that really matters.

Strategy is more complex than the profit center concept implies. A profit center is not an independent company. It does not
have the same constraints as a separate company. Nor does the independent company have the same investment opportunities it would
have as part of a balanced multidivision, multiproduct company.

Operating and administrative units of a multiproduct company
should have objectives that are considerably more complex than
those implied by reported profit. No operating unit of a multidivision company can set its own objectives properly until the corporate
strategy has defined the corporate priorities.

Cash flow control is the integrating feedback loop that supplies
the information to permit the multiproduct company to optimize
its performance. Cash flow control disregards the artificial classifica-
tions of expense and capital investments. Strategy based on cash
flow analysis focuses on the ultimate measure of performance:
"How fast is cash input compounded?" Every other factor is included in that single number if the cash is traced until it becomes
cash output.

The opportunity for the multidivision company is often very great. It has the ability to concentrate its resources where they will be the most productive. But such concentration requires a strategy specifically designed to outperform specific competitors on specific products in a specific sequence. Such strategy is not a position or posture. It is a sequence of moves.

Real success for the multiproduct company requires a company-wide coordination of sequence and timing in the deployment of resources. Failure to do this is the underlying reason why many multiproduct companies perform no better than a portfolio of unrelated investments. Success for the multidivision business depends upon organization around a strategy, not vice versa.

In the absence of an overall corporate strategy, the multidivision corporation is handicapped. It has higher overhead. It has less flexibility. It has no advantage of importance except financial reserves. This lack of strategy is formalized in the conventional profit center organizational form. Typical profit center control guarantees suboptimum objectives and performance.

A multidivision company without an overall strategy is not even as good as the sum of its parts. It is merely a portfolio of non-liquid, nontradable investments, with added overhead and constraints. Such closed-end investments properly sell at a discount from the sum of the parts. Intuition alone is an inadequate substitute for an integrated strategy.

BRINKMANSHIP IN BUSINESS

A businessman often convinces himself that he is completely logical in his behavior when in fact the critical factor is his emotional bias compared to the emotional bias of his opposition. Unfortunately, some businessmen and students perceive competition as some kind of impersonal, objective, colorless affair, with a company competing against the field as a golfer competes in medal play. A better case can be made that business competition is a major battle in which there are many contenders, each of whom must be dealt with individually. Victory, if achieved, is more often won in the mind of a competitor than in the economic arena.

I shall emphasize two points. The first is that the management of a company must persuade each competitor voluntarily to stop short of a maximum effort to acquire customers and profits. The second point is that persuasion depends on emotional and intuitive factors rather than on analysis or deduction.

The negotiator's skill lies in being as arbitrary as necessary to obtain the best possible compromise without actually destroying the basis for voluntary mutual cooperation of self-restraint. There are some common-sense rules for success in such an endeavor:

1. Be sure that your rival is fully aware of what he can gain if he cooperates and what it will cost him if he does not.
2. Avoid any action which will arouse your competitor's emotions, since it is essential that he behave in a logical, reasonable fashion.
3. Convince your opponent that you are emotionally dedicated to your position and are completely convinced that it is reasonable.

It is worth emphasizing that your competitor is under the maximum handicap if he acts in a completely rational, objective, and logical fashion. For then he will cooperate as long as he thinks he can benefit. In fact, if he is completely logical, he will not forgo the profit of cooperation as long as there is *any* net benefit.

Friendly Competitors

It may strike most businessmen as strange to talk about cooperation with competitors. But it is hard to visualize a situation in which it would be worthwhile to pursue competition to the utter destruction of a competitor. In every case there is a greater advantage to reducing the competition on the condition that the competitor does likewise. Such mutual restraint is cooperation, whether recognized as such or not.

Without cooperation on the part of competitors, there can be no stability. We see this most clearly in international relationships during times of peace. There are constant encroachments and aggressive acts. And the eventual consequence is always either voluntarily imposed self-restraint or mutual destruction. Thus, international diplomacy has only one purpose: to stabilize cooperation between independent nations on the most favorable basis possible. Diplomacy can be described as the art of being stubborn, arbitrary, and unreasonable without arousing emotional responses.

Businessmen should notice the similarity between economic competition and the peacetime behavior of nations. The object in both cases is to achieve a voluntary, cooperative restraint on the part of otherwise aggressive competitors. Complete elimination of competition is almost inconceivable. The goal of the hottest economic war is an agreement for coexistence, not annihilation. The competition and mutual encroachment do not stop; they go on forever. But they do so under some measure of mutual restraint.

"Cold War" Tactics

A breakdown in negotiations is inevitable if both parties persist in arbitrary positions which are incompatible. Yet there are major areas in business where some degree of arbitrary behavior is essential for protecting a company's self-interest. In effect, a type of brinkmanship is necessary. The term was coined to describe cold war international diplomacy, but it describes a normal pattern in business, too.

In a confrontation between parties who are in part competitors and in part cooperators, deciding what to accept is essentially emotional or arbitrary. Deciding what is attainable requires an evaluation of the other party's degree of intransigence. The purpose is to convince him that you are arbitrary and emotionally committed while trying to discover what he would really accept in settlement. The competitor known to be coldly logical is at a great disadvantage. Logically, he can afford to compromise until there is no advantage left in cooperation. If, instead, he is emotional, irrational, and arbitrary, he has a great advantage.

Conclusion

The heart of business strategy for a company is to promote attitudes on the part of its competitors that will cause them either to restrain themselves or to act in a fashion which management deems advantageous. In diplomacy and military strategy the key to success is very much the same.

The most easily recognized way of enforcing cooperation is to exhibit obvious willingness to use irresistible or overwhelming force. This requires little strategic skill, but there is the problem of convincing the competing organization that the force will be used without actually resorting to it (which would be expensive and inconvenient).

In industry, however, the available force is usually not overwhelming, although one company may be able to inflict major punishment on another. In the classic case, each party can inflict such punishment on the other. If there were open conflict, then both parties would lose. If they cooperate, both parties are better off, but not necessarily equally so — particularly if one is trying to change the status quo.

When each party can punish the other, the prospects of agreement depend on three things:

1. each party's willingness to accept the risk of punishment
2. each party's belief that the other party is willing to accept the risk of punishment
3. the degree of rationality in the behavior of each party

If these conclusions are correct, what can we deduce about how advantages are gained and lost in business competition?

First, management's unwillingness to accept the risk of punishment is almost certain to produce either the punishment or progressively more onerous conditions for cooperation — provided the competition recognized the attitude.

Second, beliefs about a competitor's future behavior or response are all that determine competitive cooperation. In other words, it is the judgment not of actual capability but of probable use of capability that counts.

Third, the less rational or less predictable the behavior of a competitor appears to be, the greater the advantage he possesses in establishing a favorable competitive balance. This advantage is limited only by his need to avoid forcing his competitors into an untenable position or creating an emotional antagonism that will lead them to be unreasonable and irrational (as he is).

Rules for the Strategist

If I were asked to distill the conditions and forces described into advice for the business-strategist, I would suggest five rules:

1. You must know as accurately as possible just what your competition has at stake in his contact with you. It is not what you gain or lose, but what he gains or loses that sets the limit on his ability to compromise with you.
2. The less the competition knows about your stakes, the less advantage he has. Without a reference point, he does not even know whether you are being unreasonable.
3. It is absolutely essential to know the character, attitudes, motives, and habitual behavior of a competitor if you wish to have a negotiating advantage.
4. The more arbitrary your demands are, the better your relative competitive position — provided you do not arouse an emotional reaction.
5. The less arbitrary you seem, the more arbitrary you can in fact be.

These rules make up the art of business brinkmanship. They are guidelines for winning a strategic victory in the minds of competitors. Once this victory has been won, it can be converted into a competitive victory in terms of sales volume, costs, and profits.

THE NONLOGICAL STRATEGY

The goal of strategy in business, diplomacy, and war is to produce a stable-relationship favorable to you with the consent of your competitors. By definition, restraint by a competitor is cooperation. Such cooperation from a competitor must seem to be profitable to him. *Any competition which does not eventually eliminate a competitor requires his cooperation to stabilize the situation.* The agreement is usually that of tacit nonaggression; the alternative is death for all but one competitor. A stable competitive situation requires an agreement between competing parties to maintain self-restraint. Such agreement cannot be arrived at by logic. It must be achieved by an emotional balance of forces. This is why it is necessary to appear irrational to competitors. For the same reason, you must seem unreasonable and arbitrary in negotiations with customers and suppliers.

Competition and cooperation go hand in hand in all real-life situations. Otherwise, conflict could only end in extermination of the competitor. There is a point in all situations of conflict where both parties gain more or lose less from peace than they can hope to gain from any foreseeable victory. Beyond that point cooperation is more profitable than conflict. But how will the benefits be shared?

In negotiated conflict situations, the participant who is coldly logical is at a great disadvantage. Logically, he can afford to compromise until there is no advantage left in cooperation. The negotiator/competitor whose behavior is irrational or arbitrary has a great advantage if he can depend upon his opponent being logical and unemotional. The arbitrary or irrational competitor can demand far more than a reasonable share and yet his logical opponent can still gain by compromise rather than breaking off the cooperation.

Absence of monopoly in business requires voluntary restraint of competition. At some point there must be a tacit agreement not to compete. Unless this restraint of trade were acceptable to all competitors, the resulting aggression would inevitably eliminate the less efficient competitors leaving only one. Antitrust laws represent a formal attempt to limit competition. All antimonopoly and fair trade laws constitute restraint of competition.

Utter destruction of a competitor is almost never profitable unless the competitor is unwilling to accept peace. In our daily social contacts, in our international affairs, and in our business affairs, we have far more ability to damage those around us than we ever dare use. Others have the same power to damage us. The implied agreement to restrain our potential aggression is all that stands between us and eventual elimination of one by the other. Both war and diplomacy are mechanisms for establishing or maintaining this self-imposed restraint on all competitors. The conflict continues, but within the implied area of cooperative agreement.

There is a definite limit to the range within which competitors can expect to achieve an equilibrium or negotiate a shift in equilibrium even by implication. Arbitrary, uncooperative, or aggressive attitudes will produce equally emotional reactions. These emotional reactions are in turn the basis for nonlogical and arbitrary responses. Thus, nonlogical behavior is self-limiting.

This is why the art of diplomacy can be described as the ability to be unreasonable without arousing resentment. It is worth remembering that the objective of diplomacy is to induce cooperation on terms that are relatively more favorable to you than to your protagonist without actual force being used.

More business victories are won in the minds of competitors than in the laboratory, the factory, or the marketplace. The competitor's conviction that you are emotional, dogmatic, or otherwise nonlogical in your business strategy can be a great asset. This conviction on his part can result in an acceptance of your actions without retaliation, which would otherwise be unthinkable. More important, the anticipation of nonlogical or unrestrained reactions on your part can inhibit his competitive aggression.

PREVENTING STRATEGY OBSOLESCENCE

There is nothing new about long-range planning, corporate strategy, or corporate development. Only the emphasis is new. By one means or another, all companies in the past have adjusted to changes in competition, markets, and technology. All companies to some degree have always had plans for improving their situation.

A few companies have been very successful, and their success rapidly brought them fame and profits. Others have had equally spectacular difficulties. For most companies, however, life has consisted of working very hard to produce small differences in performance. Yet in even the most static industries, the perspective of history reveals that different strategies eventually produce quite different consequences.

Corporate success for any company must be the result of superior use of that company's distinguishing characteristics. Yet few companies attempt to examine the strategy which brought them success in the past. Moreover, success reinforces the organization's belief in the essential correctness of past methods, philosophy, and competitive posture. So long as the underlying competitive conditions and relationships continue to hold, the corporate success may also continue. But in time these conditions must change.

This is why strategies become obsolete and inappropriate in a changing world. It is a matter of common observation that more companies seem to fall prey to creeping decline than to identifiable or specific mistakes by management in decision making.

While a persuasive case can be made that intuitive leadership was responsible for the early success of most businesses, an almost equally persuasive case can be made that this intuitive strategy cannot be extended indefinitely if:

the organization becomes large

the management generations increase

the initial environment changes substantially

The first major policy question about strategy, then, is whether an intuitive or implicit corporate strategy, defined only by the cumulative evidence of past decisions, is adequate, or whether it is necessary to have a strategy that is: (1) derived from analysis, (2) explicitly stated, (3) supported by consensus, and (4) modified by methodical reviews.

In the absence of an explicit strategy, the adaptation to changing conditions is almost certain to be deferred until past successful strategies are clearly failing. Intuitive and implied strategy adjustments are apt to be too late, too slow, and even inappropriate to cope with rapid change in a complex organization.

In complex, large-scale organizations the decision making is necessarily so diffuse that direction cannot be changed by means of individual decisions without chaos. It must be changed by changing explicit goals and approach methods (strategy) or by changing people.

The natural course of inquiry would seem to start with the present strategy, the present resources, the present competition, and the present environment. The natural pursuit of insight would seem to require an ever widening field of exploration and analysis. But for the starting point to be useful for comparison, it must be explicit:

> Why has the company succeeded against this competition in this environment?
>
> Is there a consistent pattern which constitutes a strategy?
>
> What are the critical factors for the strategy to succeed?
>
> Is there a reasonable possibility of any of these factors being significantly affected by either changes in the environment or competitive action?

Only in this fashion can the projection of past success into the future be validated.

Experience repeatedly demonstrates that conditions change and competitors take the initiative. Not only does new technology provide new means, but the whole market is constantly changing in character. Therefore, an extension of past strategy is essentially a negative course. No matter how well chosen it may be, the fact remains that sooner or later it will become inappropriate.

Still, successful strategy revision in an organization is a difficult task. The very lack of explicitness about past and current strategy and the reasons for its success can be an obstacle to accepting the need for change. High morale carries with it the implicit assumption that personal competence rather than strategic leverage is the underlying cause for superior performance. In the absence of an explicit analysis and acceptance of the strategies of the past, it is almost a foregone conclusion that any effort to change them will be regarded as an attack against those who administered them.

Underlying the entire problem of strategy formulation are pervasive difficulties of definitions, semantics, and symbols for conceptual thinking. In most business situations, there are severe constraints on the issues which may be raised. Ordinarily, decisions are made within a framework of precedent, policy, organizational responsibility, and assumptions about the purpose and nature of the business. Even the most important decisions involving capital expenditure and new product introduction are made within these bounds. The direction and character of the business are usually assumed to be unchanged. For this reason, many important strategic assumptions are accepted without question.

Another fundamental difficulty in strategic planning is that there is no inherent limit to the freedom of choice. Yet the universe is too large to explore. There is an inescapable necessity to limit the area of study to manageable proportions. But how and where? How far into the unknown must exploration go to be a reasonable investment of time and effort? When and how should this review of strategic plans take place?

As we examine these questions, it becomes clear that the role of the chief executive is far more comprehensive in the area of strategic planning than it is in the operation of the business. Whereas operating responsibilities can be delegated, strategic planning cannot. Operations can be managed by means of precedents and controls, but strategic planning requires that all decisions be treated as exceptions. Most important of all is the fact that the intuitive character of these decisions permits only the chief executive to take the initiative. For this reason, only the chief executive is within his authority in calling for a definition of strategy or in initiating a fundamental change in corporate behavior.

STRATEGIC SECTORS

A strategic sector is one in which you can obtain a competitive advantage and exploit it. Strategic sectors are defined entirely in terms of competitive differences. Strategic sector analysis performs the same function as cost effectiveness analysis. Cost effectiveness analysis optimizes value versus cost. Strategic sector analysis optimizes margin relative to competition.

Strategic sector analysis, like cost effectiveness analysis, ignores the administrative unit until the objective and its feasibility have been evaluated. The resources and the program component are assigned as necessary to administrative units in order to accomplish the mission.

Strategic sectors cut across profit centers, strategic business units, groups, divisions, departments, markets, and all other administrative units. The boundary of a strategic sector is defined by the maximum rate of change of relative competitive margin as you cross that boundary.

Strategic sectors exist because the same product can be made in many variations and supplied with many related services. Each feature and each service has a cost. But the value added by such increments varies from customer to customer. It affects product design, manufacturing capability, and distribution practices. Every change in these factors affects both cost and value simultaneously.

Design requires a focus on the strategic sector to be served. Yet every compromise of that focus either adds cost or reduces value.

Manufacture also requires a focus on the strategic sector to be served. Compromises and variety produce the same consequences on cost and value. No job shop can match the cost of a full-scale, focused factory operation.

A given strategic sector can rarely use more than one distribution channel. Since different channels have different costs and provide different services, they appeal to different customers. Therefore, customers of one channel tend to be in a different strategic sector than those served by other channels. Competitors who try to serve both strategic sectors at the same price are handicapped by a too high price in one sector and a too high cost in the other sector.

Profit centers and strategic business units are self-defeating in terms of profit unless the whole company is the profit center. GM can be the most profitable competitor because the whole company is the business unit while internal administrative units are tailored to focus on value added in strategic sectors in which they can be the largest factor.

Profit centers originated when companies became too big and complex to be managed by individual function. Decentralization, however, led to suboptimization and loss of internal financial mobility that is critical to strategic concentration.

Strategic business units were devised to reverse the effects of overfragmentation into profit centers. So-called SBUs attempted to aggregate all the strategy decisions in an administrative unit. However, the critical factor, cash flow, cannot be delegated to any SBU. If it were, then the parent would merely be a lock box holding company without strategic options as a company except divestment or acquisition.

Strategic sectors are the key to strategy because each sector's frame of reference is competition. The largest competitor in an industry can be unprofitable if the individual strategic sectors are dominated by smaller competitors. Thus, market share in the strategic sector is what determines profitability, not size of company.

THE STRATEGY REVIEW

Few companies question their strategy when all operations are profitable and successful. Success itself is the justification for continuation of the practices, policies, and patterns which brought about that success. There appears to be no need for strategy review.

When a company is in difficulty, strategy is subordinated to operations. The near-term problems of current profitability are given the highest priority. The time horizon contracts, and management performance is measured by this year's profits. There is no time for strategy review; the cost and effort appear to be an unwarranted luxury.

It would almost seem as if there is no appropriate time for a critical reappraisal of corporate strategy. Yet it is obvious that periodically the basic practices of the company must change to deal with changing conditions and competitive capabilities. If this does not happen, then the company becomes the prisoner of its own past success. It is unable to change course until unsatisfactory results make it obvious to everyone that the strategy should have been changed long before.

This pattern suggests that the success of the present must be fully understood before constructive changes can be made. It is a fact that random changes in any complex system almost invariably degrade the system performance.

The pattern also suggests that constant change in an orderly and purposeful fashion is necessary. The environment and the competition are constantly evolving, even if the company is not. These external changes will degrade performance unless the whole system is adjusted to accommodate to and take advantage of such change. The question is: "When should this review of the system as a whole occur and how can it be done?"

A strategy review is a very demanding and time-consuming task; it requires a reassessment of all underlying assumptions, and reconstruction and evaluation of all interlocking relationships. In effect, a strategy review is a system equilibrium analysis. Such analysis is a major undertaking.

Under ordinary circumstances, a company can hardly afford to question most of the characteristic policies which it follows. Too much of this kind of introspection would paralyze the ability of management to carry on everyday operations. However, at its best a strategy review does not occur as a separate event which happens periodically and is otherwise forgotten. Ideally, it is an iterative process, a sequence of theory formulation, analysis, validation, reformulation, reanalysis, and re-evaluation. If it happens this way, the critical underlying assumptions receive the attention that is required to appreciate fully their far-ranging significance. Day-by-day feedback is evaluated and checks and balances of the system are observed. The system itself is tuned. From this process a gradual evolution and upgrading can and does occur. This is probably how most strategies for an on-going business evolve. It *is* an evolution.

The process is probably primarily intuitive for most people. In this form, it has one characteristic weakness. Except under real stress, it is all too easy to be satisfied with superficial explanations and easy rationalizations. There is no pressure to analyze deeply or re-examine the underlying fundamentals.

Characteristically, intuitive insights can tolerate great inconsistencies and ambiguities no matter how brilliant or important. Fortunately, the communication and implementation of the conclusions require verbalization and discussion. This is a critical part of the rationalization of intuitive insight. Further, it leads to the exploration and testing of the whole system of relationships, not just a single facet of a relationship. This validation of various perspectives is one of the major contributions of group discussion, regardless of the decision-making process itself.

At their best, explication and reformulation lead to a full consensus of members of the organization in regard to company goals and methods. This means that the strategy becomes a part of the corporate culture. The organization is improved because the internal policies become part of the everyday knowledge of every member of the organization.

At its worst, strategy review founders on one of two extremes. At one extreme, no consensus is reached; the organization never accepts the goals; the required policies are modified beyond recognition in implementation. At the other extreme, complete acceptance of the strategy is reinforced by its success until the strategy becomes sanctified, such that questioning the strategy and its underlying assumptions becomes an attack on the organization itself.

Clearly, strategy must be under constant review; this is a demanding process in which objectivity and thoroughness are extremely difficult to achieve. Obviously, it requires a high degree of executive skill to encourage and manage the process of strategy review. This is more the art of management than the science.

A test of the mastery of this art is possible. A specific written review of strategy is a revealing exercise, as well as a record of the perspective and reasoning at a given point of time. Such a written analysis also has the great advantage of providing the focus for the discussion and depth understanding which leads to both consensus and further improvement. Discussion and communication may be far more valuable than any tangible end product.

A truly effective strategy review will answer these questions to the general satisfaction of the organization:

> Where do we put our priorities in allocating our resources in money and effort?
>
> What are the major policies that we choose to implement the strategy?
>
> What are the products and markets in which we choose to compete?
>
> What critical assumptions are we making about the competition and the environment?
>
> Exactly what do we expect to do differently or better than our competitors to be successful?

Not many companies make their strategies explicit. Not many even question their strategies in any formal fashion until they are in some difficulty. This may be changing. Explicit strategies have always been normal in areas where events characteristically move fast, such as in war and politics. Events are moving rapidly now in business, too.

An effort to review corporate strategy formally and make it specific is likely to be very frustrating and reveal considerable confusion on the subject. It can also be very much worth the effort.

BUSINESS THINKING

Business thinking starts with an intuitive choice of assumptions. Its progress as analysis is intertwined with intuition. The final choice is always intuitive. If that were not true, all problems of almost any kind would be solved by mathematicians with non-quantitative data.

The final choice in all business decisions is, of course, intuitive. It must be. Otherwise, it is not a decision, just a conclusion — a printout.

The tradeoff between subjective nonquantifiable values is by definition a subjective and intuitive choice. Intuition can be awesome in its value at times. It is known as good judgment in everyday affairs. Intuition is in fact the subconscious integration of all the experiences, conditioning, and knowledge of a lifetime, including the emotional and cultural biases of that lifetime.

But intuition alone is never enough; in fact, alone it can be disastrously wrong. Analysis, too, can be disastrously wrong. Analysis depends upon keeping the required data within manageable proportions. It also means keeping the nonquantifiable data to a minimum. Thus, analysis, by its very nature, requires initial oversimplification and an intuitive choice of initial assumptions, as well as exclusion of certain data. All of these choices are intuitive. A mistake in any one can be fatal to the analysis.

A complex problem entails a nearly infinite combination of facts and relationships. Business in particular is affected by everything, including the past, the nonlogical, and the unknowable. This complexity is compounded by multiple objectives to serve multiple constituencies, many of whose objectives must be traded off. In the face of such complexity, problem solving requires an orderly, systematic approach in order to even hope to optimize the final decision.

When the results of analysis and intuition coincide, there is little gained except confidence. When the analysis reaches conclusions that are counterintuitive, then more rigorous analysis and re-examination of underlying assumptions are always called for. The expansion of the frame of reference and the increased rigor of analysis may be fruitful.

But in nearly all problem solving there is a universe of alternative choices, most of which must be discarded without more than cursory attention. To do otherwise is to incur costs beyond the value of any solution and defer the decision to beyond the time horizon. A frame of reference is needed to screen the intuitive selection of assumptions and the relevance of data, methodology, and implicit value judgments. That frame of reference is the concept.

Conceptual thinking is the skeleton or the framework on which all the other choices are sorted out. A concept is by its nature an oversimplification. Yet its fundamental relationships are so powerful and important that they will tend to override all except the most extreme exceptions. Such exceptions are usually obvious in their importance. A concept defines a system of interactions in terms of the relative values that produce equilibrium of the system. Consequently, a concept defines the initial assumptions, the data required, and the relationships among the data inputs. In this way it permits analysis of the consequences of change in input data.

Concepts are simple in statement but complex in practice. Outputs are almost always part of the input by means of feedback. The feedback itself is consequently a subsystem interconnected with other subsystems.

Theoretically, conceptual business systems can be solved by a series of simultaneous equations. In practice, computer simulation is the only practical way to deal with the characteristic multiple inputs, feedback loops, and higher order effects in a reasonable time, at reasonable cost, and with all the underlying assumptions made explicit. Pure mathematics becomes far too ponderous.

Concepts are developed in hard science and business alike from an approximation of the scientific method. They start with a generalization of an observed pattern of experience. A concept is stated first as a hypothesis, then postulated as a theory, then defined as a decision rule. It is validated by its ability to predict. Such decision rules are often crystallized as policies. Rarely does a business concept permit sufficient proof to be called a "law," except facetiously.

Intuition disguised as status, seniority, and rank is the underlying normative mode of all business decisions. It could not be otherwise. Too many choices must be made too often. Data is expensive to collect, and is often of uncertain quality or relevance. Analysis is laborious and often far too expensive, even if only superficial.

Yet two kinds of decisions justify rigorous and painstaking analysis, guided by intuition derived from accumulated experience. The irrevocable commitment of major reserves of resources deserves such treatment. So do the major policies which guide and control the implementation of such commitments.

All rigorous analysis is inherently an iterative process. It starts with an intuitive choice and ends with an intuitive decision. The first definition of a problem must be intuitive in order to be recognized as a problem at all. The final decision is also intuitive; otherwise, there is no choice and therefore no need for decision.

Between the beginning and ending points, the rigorous process must take place. The sequence is analysis, problem redefinition, reanalysis, and then even more rigorous problem redefinition, and so forth until the law of diminishing returns dictates a halt — intuitively.

The methodology and sequence of business thinking can be stated or at least approximated as follows:

State the problem as clearly and fully as possible.

Search for and identify the basic concepts that relate to the perceived critical elements.

Define the data inputs this conceptual reference will require. Check off and identify any major factors which are not implicitly included in the conceptual base.

Redefine the problem and broaden the concept as necessary to include any such required inputs.

Gather the data and analyze the problem.

Find out to which data inputs the analysis is sensitive. Reexamine the range of options with respect to those factors and the resulting range of outputs.

Based on the insights developed by the analysis, redefine the problem and repeat the process.

Reiterate until there is a consensus that the possible incremental improvement in insight is no longer worth the incremental cost. That consensus will be intuitive. It must be, since, there is no way to know the value of the unknown.

It is a matter of common observation that much of the value of a rigorous and objective examination of a problem will be found in one of three areas:

First, the previously accepted underlying assumptions may prove to be invalid or inadequate as the problem definition is changed.

Second, the interaction among component functions may have been neglected, resulting in suboptimization by function.

Third, a previously unknown, unaccepted, or misunderstood conceptual framework may be postulated which both permits prediction of the consequence of change and partially explains these consequences.

It is also a matter of common observation that the wisest of intuitive judgments comes after full exploration of and consensus on the nature of the problem by peers with equivalent but diverse experience.

Finally, it is generally recognized that implementation of the optimum decision will prove difficult if that discussion and consensus have not been continued long enough to make the relationship between the overall objective and the specific action seem clear to all who must interpret and implement the required policies. Otherwise, the intuition of those who do the implementation will be used to redefine the policies which emerged from analysis. This is one reason why planned organizational change is so difficult, and random drift is so common.

Here are some fundamental procedural suggestions. Define the problem and hypothesize the approach to a solution intuitively before wasting time on data collection and analysis. Do the first analysis lightly. Then, and only then, redefine the problem more rigorously and reanalyze in depth. (Don't go to the library and read all the books before you know what you want to learn.) Use mixed project research teams composed of some people with finely honed intuitions from experience and others with highly developed analytical skills but too little experience to know what cannot be done. Perhaps in this way you can achieve the best of both analysis and intuition in combination and offset the weaknesses of each.

II

CORPORATE ORGANIZATION

2

ORGANIZATION

The "new biology" promises a new insight into organizational structure and behavior. The human race and business have had a great deal of experience in organization. But our organization theories are mostly either folklore or intuitive rationalization. Our constant preoccupation with organization reflects its importance. It also reflects the lack of a satisfactory basis for evaluation.

The new biology is in the hypothesis stage. It is radical. It is controversial. It is still suspect to many academicians. Yet it makes good common sense. Darwin, Freud, Pavlov, Taylor, Rothlisberger, McGregor, and Barnard may all be right and their views compatible.

We can learn from human history and from biological comparisons. The apostles are Lorenz, Morris, and Ardrey.

Humans, like all creatures, are born with certain innate patterns of behavior. The most basic are called instincts. Others are so natural they are learned almost effortlessly. All of these patterns tend to be a predisposition to behave in certain ways. Most can be traced to behavioral patterns that in the past had survival value for the species, not just for the individual. The Darwinian concept of survival of the fittest individual does not explain everything. The fittest species survive too. Each species shares a common gene pool.

The two most universally observable patterns are "rank ordering" and the "territorial imperative." These are interrelated.

Rank ordering is sometimes called "the pecking order." Specifically, it is the sequence in which the members of a social group will accept initiative from others. The Alpha accepts initiative from no one, but everyone accepts initiative from the Alpha. The exact opposite is true for the Omega. In between, each member will accept initiative from those above in rank, but not from those below. Rank ordering seems to be essential to a very large portion of high-order species, particularly those social animals which live and work in groups.

Rank ordering is a status system. Without it, there would be no cooperation; coordination would be impossible. Someone must decide and initiate; others must accept and cooperate.

The military learned about rank ordering early because it had to do so to survive. But rank ordering is common among all social creatures which live together, whether a flock of geese, a troop of monkeys, or a modern corporation.

The importance of rank ordering seems to depend upon the need for cooperation and the hostility of the environment. The more hostile the environment, the stronger the rank ordering. The more cooperation that is needed, the stronger the rank ordering. Those species which do not have rank ordering live a very, very lonely life.

The territorial imperative is equally pervasive. Fish, birds, and mammals protect territories against their own species. The closer they are to the center of their territory, the stronger they become. The further away they are, the less aggressive and the weaker they become. Thus, territorial size and boundaries tend to become a measure of relative strength. Territory and rank are also often intimately associated with each other.

Territorial boundaries do not usually matter except with respect to members of the same species. Territories are often held by groups against other groups, as well as by the individual against other individuals.

Competition for rank or territory often takes the form of ritual behavior rather than actual combat. These symbolic battles are conventional ways of competing; anything else would be "unfair." Symbolic ritual competition settles the issue without destruction of the contestants.

Social groups have a characteristic, most effective size. In the distant past this may have been determined by how and what man hunted as well as how well he could know and predict the behavior of his peers. Today it seems to indicate that work groups of seven to twelve members are the most likely to be efficient and effective teams.

There are innate predispositions in man to behave in certain ways. Deep in the history of mankind are reasons why these patterns were superior ways to survive. The inclinations still exist.

Human organization in the future will be better and more effective. We can learn from our own past. As we understand better what we are, we can apply our reason to make use of our new knowledge.

There is nothing in business with which mankind has had more experience than organization. Yet new insights from the new biology may overturn much of our conventional wisdom about organizational behavior.

USES OF POWER

The first use of power is to preserve and compound it. All other uses of power are incidental.

Man's deepest instincts focus on a single command derived from millennia in the jungle: "Know your environment and control it." This drive displays itself in two forms, the territorial imperative and the rank ordering process.

The territorial imperative says "Our group is stable and safe only if we protect it from all outsiders whom we are unable to control." In the corporation the outsider can be someone who is outside of the work group, their function, or their environment, or merely someone they do not know well enough. But territorial protection must be a group activity to be effective. Group activity requires coordinated cooperation. Coordination is impossible unless someone has the initiative and will habitually be respected.

The rank ordering process determines where the initiative will be respected. Rank is the measure of acceptable initiative. The organizational name for this is status. Status is the power to control your environment internally.

Power is the ability to initiate activity for others and to disregard others' initiatives. The power can be used to strengthen power. The usual mechanism in human affairs is a system of favors. It ranges from being neighborly to congressional log-rolling. It is in constant use in the simple social activities of everyday life.

Favors are used to reward. Favors also are used to punish by reducing the initiative available to others. Giving or withholding favors is the lever of organizational power.

Favors are organizational currency. I do something for you that costs me, personally, less than it is worth to you. Later I can call on you for a favor that costs you less than it is worth to me. If I can invest the net proceeds in additional favors, then I can compound a power base.

Unfortunately, within an organization most favors are provided at the expense of the organization, not the individual. Personal power maintenance is an extremely expensive hidden overhead. Most corporate staff costs far more than its apparent cost. Most staff is dependent upon status for its very survival. This is why most public governing bodies rapidly become corrupt in the absence of effective measures of performance of duty. This is also why ambiguous objectives and ill defined objectives can eventually be utterly destructive to any organization's performance.

Yet all organizations must have a working system of mutual favors which holds the cooperative system together. Otherwise, each part of the organization becomes the mortal enemy of the strangers in other parts who are inevitably crowded into violating the territorial imperative. But unless the external needs of the organization for survival and success clearly require the subordination of personal ambition, then the resources of the entire organization will gradually become subordinated to the preservation of personal rank.

The executive must choose between using his power to strengthen the organization and using his power to strengthen his personal power base. If the organization is under no pressure, the diversion of resources will be seen as a perogative of high rank and status. If, on the other hand, the organization's needs are clear and pressing, any diversion of resources to unrelated purposes will be seen as an abdication of leadership. The real basis for status is the importance of the activity to the organization. That is the underlying reason why initiative will be accepted and supported. Actions which use corporate resources for activities unimportant to the organization tend to destroy the basis of rank and status.

This is why the corporate politician flourishes and saps the strength of the whole organization, unless strategy is explicit, goals are clear and relevant, and strong leadership is guided by objectives that are valued by everyone in the organization.

Power must be used to obtain performance. But the only way the abuse of power can be inhibited or prevented is to make sure that such abuse is seen as dysfunctional. Status is destroyed by actions which are considered contrary to the common purpose. Misuse of power will be seen as misuse, however, only if the objectives and the reasons for them are abundantly clear.

The corporation without an explicit strategy will fall into the hands of politicians.

WHY CHANGE IS SO DIFFICULT

Success in the past always becomes enshrined in the present by the overvaluation of the policies and attitudes which accompanied that success. As long as the environment and competitive behavior do not change, these beliefs and policies contribute to the stability of the firm.

However, with time these attitudes become embedded in a system of beliefs, traditions, taboos, habits, customs, and inhibitions which constitute the culture of the firm. Such cultures are as distinctive as the cultural differences between societies or the personality differences between individuals. They cannot be changed very easily. Indeed any effort to change them is quite likely to be viewed as an attack upon the organization itself.

These observations are a matter of common experience. For example, sharp and painful adjustments are required when two comparable organizations merge, because of inevitable differences in corporate style and culture. Also, when a new chief executive is appointed from outside the organization, one of two actions will follow. Either there will be a long period with little change while he gets to "know" the organization, or there will be a period of considerable stress and perhaps personnel turnover while a new corporate culture evolves.

These problems of change cannot be avoided; all organizations, like all organisms, must adapt to changes in their environment or die. All organizations do change when put under sufficient pressure. This pressure must be either external to the organization or the result of very strong leadership.

It is rare for any organization to generate sufficient pressure internally to produce significant change in direction. Indeed, internal pressure is likely to be regarded as a form of dissatisfaction with the organization's leadership. To change by evolution rather than revolution, the change must not only be tolerated but actively guided and directed in very explicit terms by the leadership of the firm.

In this process the corporate leadership faces major dilemmas. The organization's investment in the status quo is always a heavy one. This is almost inherent in the definition of a culture. Changes in policy and strategy are threatening, producing a whole series of changes in objectives, values, status values and hierarchy. Jobs, rank and many cherished beliefs are put into jeopardy.

Most of the organization is not in a position to see the need for policy and organizational change until long after the optimum time for action has passed. Corporate culture tends to obscure the need for change until the organization as a whole can accept the reality of the need. But when the need is so obvious that the whole organization can recognize it, competitive advantage in flexibility and speed of response has been lost.

On the other hand, if an effort is made to introduce change before there is a general awareness of the need, the very ability to lead is endangered. Any fundamental change in corporate policy is almost certain to be regarded by a significant part of the organization as irrational. No matter how sound the change may be, it is at some point rooted in an intuitive concept of the relative values of a complex of factors affecting the future. There will always be a large part of the organization which does not perceive these values in the same way. These people will therefore consider the change unwarranted and will question the leadership's ability to make "reasonable" decisions.

It is obvious, as well, that major changes in policy have far-reaching consequences that dictate caution and conservatism. The attitude toward change is always conservative or reactionary until both the reasons for the change and the consequences are clearly defined. This is an impossible set of preconditions for most policy changes. Any significant change produces a train of interrelated and often unanticipated corollary changes. Each policy has been keyed to others and changes in one requires a re-evaluation of the related policies. Too much change in policies leads to a complete restructuring of the corporate edifice, with all the cost and confusion incident to any major reconstruction.

Not only the organization, but the leadership itself, incurs considerable risk by changing policy. By definition, a policy is applied to decisions in the future. To be valid the policy must be based upon assumptions about future conditions and competition. These assumptions, in turn, are based upon others. At some point the information needed to make a decision becomes so problematical and conditional that further fact finding and analysis are unrewarding, and the decision becomes intuitive.

Such decisions on major issues constitute a severe risk of exposure. The apparent verities of the past successes must be abandoned for unproven policies based upon uncertain data. To the risk of failure from incorrect choice must be added the risk of failure in leadership because the organization does not see the need for the change. Even the most wisely chosen risks may still prove to be fatal to the current leadership if the consequences cannot be proved in fact.

All the forces of corporate culture are set against change. Yet the rewards can be substantial for the management with strong enough leadership both to anticipate the change required and to manage the evolution. The competitive advantages of superior strategy will only be available if management can make major shifts in policy early enough for the need or the purpose not to be obvious to the organization as a whole or to its competitors.

Thus, there are at least three major requirements for management to outperform the competition. The first is to conceive and make explicit a superior strategy. The second is to provide the leadership needed to overcome the obstacles to change. The third, and often critical, requirement is to provide that leadership at a time when the organization as a whole would ordinarily oppose the necessary changes.

LEADERSHIP

There are three fundamentally different executive functions. The first is preservation of the organization. The second is control of organizational response to deviation from expectations. The third is planning future expectations. All of these are made possible by the personal qualities of leadership.

The essence of leadership is the ability to change the organization's conception of ideal performance. The strength of leadership can be measured by the rate at which these ideals are changed. The quality of leadership is reflected by the wisdom used in choosing the new ideals. The initial test of leadership skill is in the choice of the inescapable compromise between speed of change and security of the leader's ability to lead.

Management can be distinguished from leadership. The management function deals with what the organization ought to do, whereas the leadership function deals with the motivation of the organization to do that which it ought to do. Normally, the two functions are so interrelated that the differences are not recognized even by the leader-manager himself. However, in very strong leader-manager combinations, the difference may become apparent to the leader-manager because of the obvious compromise required between what good management dictates and what continued leadership will permit.

Both good management and strong leadership require clearly defined goals and objectives. Good management will produce worthy goals, and good leadership will rapidly obtain organizational acceptance of and motivation to attain these goals.

In a business organization, good and strong leaders will do these things:

1. Gain complete and willing acceptance of their leadership.
2. Determine those business goals, objectives, and standards of behavior which are as ambitious as the potential abilities of the organization will permit.
3. Introduce these objectives and motivate the organization to accept them as their own. The rate of introduction will be the maximum consistent with continued acceptance of leadership. Because of this need for acceptance, the new manager must always go slowly, except in emergencies. In emergencies the boss *must not* go slowly if he is to maintain leadership.
4. Change the organizational relationships internally as necessary to facilitate both the acceptance and attainment of the new objectives.

Some managers never make the first hurdle of acceptance as the leader of their organization. They may manage but they do not lead. Their organization fights them on every change. They are told only that which they ask. Their followers feel that "The boss doesn't understand."

Before a leader can lead he must first belong. More than anyone else, he must live up to the ideals and standards the group has already accepted. If he cannot do this, he cannot lead, no matter what his ability or power. For these reasons, leaders are strong or weak only with reference to specific groups. The leader leads only that group which will accept him first as a member and then as first among them.

Other managers fail as strong leaders even though they are fully accepted as leaders. They fail because they do not lead anywhere. They conform to the group's norms and standards; in fact, they defend and preserve the status quo. Their leadership can remain secure provided the group standards do not call for the leader to promote or initiate change. With such a manager, the leadership survives but the organization eventually dies because of its failure to adapt to a changing world.

Some managers are accepted as leaders and actively lead their organization, but they still fail because of faulty or inadequate goals and objectives. This is an intellectual failure, not a spiritual one, due to lack of managerial vision, not lack of courage or willingness. It is one of the most difficult kinds of managerial failure to detect because the strength of leadership hides its own weakness.

Partial failure is also common in cases where leadership is accepted and vigorous, and goals are wisely chosen. These leaders fail because of less than optimum choice between rate of progress and leadership security. This failure is not absolute; it is a comparative failure. It is a failure to do as well as it is possible to do. The leader who leads too rapidly loses his leadership, the one who leads too slowly just does not get there as fast. As in racing, the stress on the driver is very great at maximum speeds. Most leaders just do not take the risks required for maximum results. Many do not attempt anything like maximum performance because of the stress and strain they experience.

Even when a leader has done everything else, he may fall short of the best possible performance because of failure to adapt organizational relationships to the current objectives, needs, and resources. This, again, is a technical handicap in a comparative sense rather than an absolute failure. It is a removable limitation on performance. However, the correct decision is highly intuitive and subjective. The ideal organization, even in a static situation with idealized people, would be difficult enough to formulate; with flesh-and-blood people in a dynamic situation, the optimum organization relationships are virtually unknowable.

The inevitable cost of change and the temporary loss in effectiveness must be balanced against the desired benefits. The disturbance in the informal relationships will certainly reduce the leader's acceptance and control, at least temporarily. The benefits sought are based upon the projected behavior of people who can never be fully predictable. These benefits will be effective at a time in the future when the situation may be quite different from that now visualized. The net advantage of organizational change is thus most difficult to determine and the known costs are usually great. Therefore, many leaders cling to the known at the risk of falling short of their optimum performance.

Being an effective leader and manager has some of the same requirements as being a winning poker player. A knowledge of the odds is indispensable. Ability to sense others' attitudes is also indispensable. Adequate working capital must be acquired before any major risks can be taken. Choosing a proper balance in calculating risk versus reward is essential.

Good management sees the opportunity and what must be done to grasp it. Good leadership chooses the right timing and speed of implementation while developing an organization that not only can but wants to achieve those objectives.

THE CHIEF EXECUTIVE'S PERSPECTIVE

Ordinarily, the day-to-day demands on top executive time require a large amount of effort to perform the ceremonial functions. For example, anyone who reads the daily reports on the activities of the chief executive of the United States cannot help wondering when he has any time left for business. Equally pressing are the demands for controlling the organization. Some call this "fire fighting" — solving the ever-present problems of operation.

Only after the needs of operating and controlling the organization have been satisfied is there any time available for planning the future. Yet it is precisely in the growth planning area that there is no substitute or delegate who can replace the chief executive. In this area not only his decisions but his leadership are critical.

The chief can concentrate on either what needs to be done or how to get the organization to do it. One requires strategy, the other leadership. This commentary focuses on the chief executive as leader rather than as strategist.

The Chief Executive as Obstacle

The chief executive himself is often the main obstacle to growth:

He gives priority to other interests by his own attention.

He takes a short-term point of view which excludes the initiatives necessary for longer term growth.

He discourages initiatives that do not come from him or his close associates.

He preserves the traditional corporate mythology as the basis for all strategy discussion.

These kinds of behavior are often so paralyzing that only a major crisis or threat can temporarily unshackle the real corporate strengths. In any case, if there is to be growth, it must occur because the chief is a leader, not just a trustee.

The crucial fact to recognize is that these executive inhibitions merely demonstrate the pervasive effects of the chief executive's office. These are not decisions, they are just attitudes — the attributes of leadership — which can be positive or negative.

Direction of Growth

No amount of staff work, discussion, participation, or analysis will result in a coordinated effort by the organization unless it derives from a conviction at the top. Thus, the indispensable contribution of the chief executive is a sense of direction. From anyone else, this direction is merely controversy and conjecture. Without this sense of direction, the organization will inevitably divide into cliques and schools of thought — canceling out its own best efforts. A good leader works towards organizational consensus, gets it, and then implements it. But he is out in front when the action is needed.

One question that executives frequently ask is: "What does the old man really want?" Once that is made clear, the response can be taken for granted in most companies.

Unfortunately, many chief executives get more satisfaction from fire fighting and solving problems of control than they do from the challenges of strategy development. To them, "long-range planning" is academic and suspect. The truly critical decisions are thus apt to be easily neglected since the real purpose of long-range planning is to do now what is necessary to secure opportunities in the future.

Yet it is obvious that no one in the company can safely take the initiative in committing resources to the future unless he knows where the top management wants the company to go and what it is willing to do to get there.

A Basic Dilemma

A corporation is a culture. The chief is its leader. To be effective, he must know what is happening and also know the sentiments of his subordinates. To do this, he must allow them to participate as fully as possible in his decision making. Yet this participation is self-limiting because it is very time-consuming. There is a fundamental conflict between the need for communication and participation on one hand, and the need for efficiency on the other. This is a real test of executive leadership.

The Chief as Leader

The basic role of the chief executive is as the leader of an organization. He sets the goals; establishes the value system; distributes the rewards; and determines rank and status within the organization. In this way, he provides both direction and motivation. He can confer status; he can confer authority; he can provide influence.

All of this is merely a means of focusing attention on those things which he feels deserve priority. The chief must be a leader first, no matter where he leads. Otherwise, he is ineffectual.

Ingrown Leadership

Unfortunately, many chief executives focus their attention on purely internal relationships. Elaborate controls are used, based on the assumption that the important events are inside, not outside. However, controls do not explain performance. They only signal deviation from expectations.

The significant questions concern the reasons why either good or bad performance should be expected. Companies which cannot fully explain their current performance are not ready to plan their future.

Growth Goals

Growth goals can focus on either the end result or the means to be used. Focusing on a goal such as X percent per year means very little when taken alone. Focusing on the difference between a conservative extrapolation of the present compared to the future goal may delineate the magnitude of the problem, but it does not help solve it. Focusing on the means is more useful but still inadequate, because there are many opportunities but only limited resources.

Proper growth planning sets realistic goals and explicitly states the means to be used for attaining them. In doing this, it is fatal to be too optimistic and it is defeatist to be too conservative. Overly optimistic goals not only destroy morale but authorize the expenditure of resources and effort toward goals that will not be attained even though the expense is incurred. Excessive conservatism merely means lost opportunity and a weakened competitive position.

The limit on realistic goals is set by the ability to identify and concentrate on business areas where the company has both a competitive advantage and where change is taking place. Both conditions must be present. Without a competitive advantage, there is unlikely to be any profit. Without a changing situation, there is little opportunity to displace entrenched competition. Ordinarily, this change is easiest to identify in a growing market, but it can also occur in a shrinking market, or during a technical shift or another kind of change.

Goals and Evaluation of Division Performance

Goals must be realistic for another reason. If they are not, the whole control system, as well as corporate leadership is endangered. This is almost axiomatic, particularly for divisional officers.

Divisional officers have a different perception than corporate officers. The corporate officers represent the divisional officers' final court of judgment. A division head is constantly comparing risk and the potential of improved performance, evaluating them in terms of corporate management expectations, not necessarily in terms of his own assessment of the corporation's best interests. Any change inherently involves risk. Therefore, his decision is always tempered by his assessment of the possibility of achieving goals versus the risk required to try.

Overly optimistic goals nearly always result in one of two extremes. If the goal is seen as a must, then the division manager must "go for broke." This can result in reckless risk taking. More commonly, the unrealistic goal results in the ultraconservative action. The reasoning here is: "Why take any chances to achieve an unattainable goal?"

Executive Leadership

The decisions of the chief executive are important, often critical. Yet in a sense they may not even be a reason for concern, provided the chief is effective as a leader.

As a leader he focuses attention on the corporate purposes and the strategic decisions. If he does this well enough, he will also, in the process, support the staff work and analysis needed for him to be able to make his own decisions from knowledge and with wisdom.

If he is a strong leader he will produce a strong organization. A strong organization requires considerable leadership but its managers need few decisions to be made for them. It is the weak leader with the weak organization who must make all of the decisions because he has been unable to obtain concensus on goals and the means of attaining them.

Strong leadership communicates very well the goals, aspirations, and values of top management. This communication, however, is based upon excellent upward communication of information about risks, results, plans, concepts, capabilities, competition, and the environment. Leadership cannot be strong unless it is realistic.

Leaders must lead. To do so they must both listen and make decisions. When they do, they must communicate goals and exercise controls. They are and must be the chief strategists because, in leading, they necessarily allocate the corporate resources in anticipation of its future behavior.

The Chief Executive and Rate of Change

A serious attempt on the part of the chief executive to alter traditional practices can create problems. Out of his efforts generally emerges the necessity of rethinking many of the key assumptions held by the members of the organization. Also, it is frequently necessary for the chief executive to rethink his own contribution to the company.

No chief executive can transform an existing organization into his heart's desire in a short time. To accomplish this would require, in effect, the death of the existing social structure and tradition within the organization and the rebirth of a new society. It is interesting to note that true revolutionaries do exactly that — with great loss of effectiveness in the transition period (e.g., Cuba under Castro).

If the company is of any size the chief executive cannot *impose* a particular concept of the future on the organization. Indeed, many tales of corporate catastrophe stem from the president entertaining a vision of the future which the remainder of the company neither understood nor was in a position to support.

Still, the chief executive has the greatest influence on the organization. Unless he accepts the responsibility for creating a direction which others will accept, the company cannot really influence its own evolution.

By the nature of his position, the chief executive should be the best informed person in the organization as well as the person in the best position to communicate to the organization as a whole. No other person has the right or the responsibility to take the initiative on such a comprehensive scale.

The chief must take the lead if there is to be corporate growth in a changing environment. There are some aspects of leadership that cannot be delegated. In matters of strategy and corporate growth, the chief executive stands alone. He cannot delegate. He alone must make that ultimate decision on corporate direction. Failure here is abdication.

THE PRICE OF UNCERTAINTY

Few things can paralyze an organization more than uncertainty about the strategy and the value system of the chief executive. Such uncertainty paralyzes initiative, inhibits adaptation to change, and makes long-range planning impossible.

Many of the committee meetings, staff conferences, and even ceremonial occasions within a company serve primarily to reinforce and strengthen the assurance that "these are our objectives; this is how we propose to reach them; that is the area in which initiative will be acceptable." In the absence of such reassurance, initiative is a very dangerous thing.

A manager cannot afford to propose too often courses of action which will be rejected. Nor can he afford, even once, to start on a major plan or program which at some point in the future will be dependent upon uncertain management support or approval. The intermediate manager who leads his subordinates in a plan of action which will be vetoed at a critical phase of implementation seriously jeopardizes his own future acceptability as a leader and a manager of his subordinates.

All plans imply a sequence of events over time. In business all plans of consequence require coordinated activities by numbers of people. The people must be able to predict each other's future behavior. This mutual dependence upon predictability applies across the organization, of course. However, it applies up and down the chain of command to such an extent that the entire organization's performance is dependent upon it.

These mutual expectations become highly codified and are reinforced by ritual and tradition in organizations which must be both highly coordinated and quickly responsive to a changeable and hostile environment. The military services offer textbook examples of this pattern.

On the other hand, there are many organizations in which little coordination is needed between the major parts. In such organizations the freedom of initiative and the boundaries of that initiative become equally well established and scrupulously observed. Most universities recognize this need for a clear understanding of the limits on interference with initiative. "Academic freedom" is thus reflected in organizational form as well as pedagogical philosophy.

The classic one-man organization has the great advantage that eventually everyone gets to know exactly what the boss believes and how he will react. However, one-man organizations nearly always fail when initiative is required by someone other than the boss. This is the reason one-man organizations almost always get into trouble when the nature of the operation requires decentralization and multiple initiative.

There is a genuine dilemma here. The chief must either make all the decisions or be completely predictable. Yet he cannot make all the decisions because the channels of communication are too limited, almost by definition. Neither can he be predictable because, by definition, that *does* mean he can make no decisions except those already predicted.

The solution to this organizational dilemma lies in policy. A policy is a statement of how a class of decisions will be made. Therefore, a policy decision removes the need for the multiple decisions that would otherwise be required if each one were considered separately. The value of policies is that they remove uncertainty. Without them no one would dare take the initiative except in routine and repetitive areas.

The art of policy making is one of the most difficult and essential in business. Good policies are difficult to make because they require that all of the objectives and plans of the organization be taken into account.

In the absence of policy, all initiative is reserved for the chief executive. Corporate performance, therefore, is limited by the availability and efficiency of communication with the chief. Truly decentralized or diverse operations become impossible in the absence of policy unless the chief is so weak that he cannot control the organization, or the organization needs no coordination at all.

The starting point of good policy is a well-defined, clearly understood, and reasonably explicit corporate strategy. Even brilliant, intuitive, *ad hoc* improvisation is no substitute for this. The required sequence, then, for business performance is as follows:

Strategy formulation and setting of objectives. These two tasks are inextricable from each other.

Development of long-range plans for strategy implementation.

Formulation of appropriate policies.

Leadership.

Absence of any one of these elements can lead to the uncertainty which can paralyze the organization.

STRATEGY PLANNING IN THE
MULTIDIVISIONAL FIRM: (The Role of
the Chief Executive)

Most of the conventional ideas that we have about the contribution of the chief executive to corporate management suffer
from historical obsolescence. Developed in the context of a company
that was in only one business, they are of little help in coming to
grips with questions such as these:

> How can the chief executive gain the consensus of a group of
> division managers operating in widely different fields about
> some overall corporate purpose? Should he even try?
>
> How can the chief executive evaluate division managers who
> operate in fields they know better than he?
>
> How can the chief executive guide the allocation of resources
> in a diversified company?
>
> In what terms can the future of a diversified company be
> meaningfully expressed? Is it all encompassed in the concept
> of return on investment?

Diversification is a widespread condition in American industry.
It is also an accelerating trend. There are compelling economic arguments for a company being — or becoming — diversified. At some
point, additional diversification probably represents an increasing
burden, rather than a growing strength. That point will differ from
one company to the next, depending on the managerial mechanisms
which it contains, and the style in which they are operated.

The management of a diversified organization carries with it
fundamental changes in the nature of the chief executive's role.
And changes in managerial style are much more difficult to accomplish than broadening the product line or negotiating the acquisition
of additional divisions. Looking at the performance of widely diversified companies, once can draw the conclusion that the problems
these firms experience in making effective use of their total resources
more than counterbalance their financial strengths and put them at
a disadvantage compared with more sharply focused companies.

The major strategic issues in multidivisional firms relate to
the achievement of collective strength. Where there is no specific
advantage to the divisions being associated with one another, there is

no justification for them to march under the same corporate banner. A significant strategy problem is, therefore, identification of the real advantages of association and the directions in which these can be best exploited.

The role of the chief executive in the multidivisional firm is largely one of strategic planning. His major concerns are related to the formulation of corporate objectives and the program for achieving them. Only through his leadership can the corporate future be more than an agglomeration of individual divisional operations.

PROFIT CENTERS AND
DECENTRALIZED MANAGEMENT

The idea of profit centers and decentralization often gets in the way of good management if the idea is taken very seriously. Such ideas are often not what they seem.

Many companies which profess decentralization do not really have it. Profit centers are not necessarily so — if overall corporate profit performance is being optimized. Independent profit centers are by definition neither independent nor profit centers if, in fact, there is any significant mutual interaction or synergy between cost centers.

There are several ambiguities involved. They grow out of the underlying assumptions and implications in the words "profit center" and "decentralization."

First, there is the implication that absolute level of profit is a measure of management's current performance. It may be nothing of the kind. The near-term absolute level of profit may reflect a long series of previous management decisions. It may also represent a conscious decision either to increase heavy "expense investment" for the future or, conversely, to liquidate past "expense investment." All investment and deferred benefits cannot be capitalized.

Second, there is the implication that profit can be the measure of divisional performance in a multiunit company. This is seldom the case. If there is any mutual support between divisions, then the resulting benefits are necessarily windfalls to one division or the other, when compared to an independent operation, and are largely beyond the influence of divisional management.

Third, there is the implication that each profit center should optimize its own profit, when obviously it is the total profit of the corporation that should be optimized. Most unit managers are faced sooner or later with the conflict between improving their own unit's reported performance and improving overall corporate performance. Often there are many circumstances which require the apparent unit performance to be depressed in order to optimize the corporate overall performance.

Finally, there is the implication that profit centers can be measured and evaluated as if they were separate companies. This is hardly defensible if there is, in fact, good reason for the separate units to be grouped together.

Profit centers and decentralized management have become almost a hallmark of American business organization. The underlying philosophy is that authority and responsibility should be parallel. Further, there is the implication that in a complex business the authority, and therefore, responsibility, must inevitably be delegated. These principles *are* valid — but only to the point where they conflict with the principle that overall management should optimize overall performance.

The justification for central management in a diversified company must always be that it can produce results superior to those that a decentralized organization would produce if left completely alone. This means that a central management must impose constraints on the direction of decentralized operations.

The best balance between centralization and decentralization must be far more effective than either extreme. At the same time, this balance requires a much higher level of management sophistication than the simpler modes. The necessary conditions are easily stated although hard to achieve.

To achieve this balance, the goals and potential of the organization as a whole must be clearly understood by the corporate management. This means that the corporation must have a well-defined and explicit strategy. Those who make decisions of consequence must either understand this overall corporate strategy in all of its complexity or be subject to policy constraints which effectively limit choice to decisions which are compatible with the overall strategy. When this has been done, then each decision should be delegated to that part of the organization which is in the fullest possession of all the relevant information.

Left alone, each profit center should be expected to maximize its own value system. It is the central authority's responsibility to optimize the combination of profit centers. However, it can do this only by one of two approaches. The first, and more obvious, approach is to supervise closely the operation and internal policy of each profit center. By definition, this is not decentralization. It also implies a centralization of wisdom.

The other alternative is to optimize the system by depressing one profit center's performance in order to achieve an improvement in other profit centers. This is highly desirable and laudable, but it distorts the performance measurement of all the profit centers. The direct use of profitability as a performance measure is immediately undermined. Thus, overall optimization also implies a restricted definition of decentralization.

There is a wide range of degrees of freedom which are possible within the concept of decentralization. Listed below in descending degrees of freedom are some examples:

1. Parent company is essentially an investment portfolio custodian (regardless of corporate form).

2. Parent company is in effect a holding company which serves as a board of directors in setting policy for the individual operations.

3. Parent company, in addition, provides common financial resources to each operation in accordance with overall corporate policy.

4. Parent company actively participates in strategy development and policy formulation for operating units.

5. Parent company coordinates some key activity or activities — for example, in a common sales organization.

6. Parent company provides detailed policy direction of operations in all major activities.

7. Parent company also makes key operating decisons.

These various parent-division roles require differing degrees of internal communication and specialization in the decision-making process. This is another way of describing internal organizational form.

All practical basic organizational forms for complex operations have certain common characteristics:

centralized policy direction based on explicit strategy concepts

decentralized administration of operations based on complex, not simple, operating standards and expectations

mechanisms of communication and review which keep both strategy and operating objectives realistically related to each other

a quality of leadership which achieves consensus on both strategy implementation and operating standards

Profit centers and decentralization connote an oversimplified description of this set of organizational relationships.

Some form of decentralized operation is and always will be essential for any business of substantial size. There are many reasons why multiproduct organizations are more efficient in the use of their resources than a single-product organization. In fact, virtually all corporations of any consequence sell more than one product. However, as the variety and breadth of product time increases, then the degree of relatedness of synergy among products decreases.

It is obvious that management techniques, style, and organization must be modified as products and markets become more numerous and diverse. If this is not done, then size and diversity eventually become handicaps instead of advantages. The management organization and policies must be tailored to the individual combination of products, markets, and people.

For each company there is an optimum organization and set of policies which is superior to centralized management with its inflexibility, bureaucracy, slow response, and insensitivity; and also superior to fully decentralized profit centers which act independently of their potential for mutual reinforcement.

THE STORY OF JOE (A Fable)

Joe made himself quite a reputation as a "turn-around" manager. It began when he was put in charge of a very sick division of his large and diversified company. Within a couple of years he changed it from a big loser to a modest profit maker.

He turned around sick divisions not once, but several times. His staff thought he was the best. The corporate management eulogized him. Morale in his operations was high. But Joe's reputation began to tarnish.

After Joe left these divisions and turned them over to someone else, they seemed to go sour. They dropped back slowly and inexorably into their former unprofitability. Each of the managers who succeeded Joe convinced top management that major new investment was necessary if the sick operation was ever to be built into something really worthwhile. The suspicion grew that Joe had not really "turned around" those operations.

By then Joe was a high ranking officer of this great company. Joe was put in charge of one of the company's very large divisions which, over many years, seemed to fail to realize its promise. Under Joe nothing changed. He tried hard. But nothing changed. He tightened budgets. He cut overhead. He looked for every penny he could save. All this had been done before. Joe failed. This operation continued to sink slowly into mediocrity.

So Joe was fired. It wasn't done lightly. Joe had been a hardworking and loyal employee. No one could find fault with what he had done. He had seemed to be a first-class manager. Yet the facts were clear for all to see. Every operation that Joe managed looked good for awhile but became a disaster eventually. Joe was really bad news.

Some of the younger managers in the company were greatly disturbed. How could Joe look so good and turn out like that? Joe had seemed to be a good man, a good manager, a good businessman, a leader. Why . . . ? So the young men sought out a retired old-timer wise in the ways of people and corporations. They asked him why. And this is what he told them.

"Business is complex. Nobody is really sure what determines success. The only thing that seems sure is results. The bottom right-hand corner of the P&L statement seems real. But it is not real either. It is based on a whole series of assumptions about the future which have been stylized as accounting.

"Joe's company believed its own accounting. It set Joe's goals in short-term budgets. It asked Joe to make those accounts show a profit and do it quickly. Joe did it.

"Joe cut out every expense that didn't have an immediate payback. He cut back on advertising, product development, maintenance, personnel development, training, and all support activities not absolutely essential.

"Joe liquidated every asset he could which had a depreciation charge in excess of current contribution. This not only improved the return on the remaining assets but reduced his excess capacity and left mostly assets with low book values. This was done very early when Joe took charge, since early writeoffs can always be attributed to your predecessor.

"Joe then held prices firm and perhaps a little on the high side. This tended slowly to lose market share, but then customers do not ordinarily shift suppliers very fast. Meantime, a few percentage points in margin looked very good in a marginal operation.

"Joe did exactly what he should have done. He did exactly what the company's control system asked him to do. He did exactly what the company's incentive plans rewarded.

"Far beyond that in importance, Joe did exactly what the company *should* have wanted him to do. Joe initiated an orderly liquidation of those businesses which should have been liquidated because they were too poorly situated to really compete."

So why did Joe get fired?

"Joe did what he was told to do, but the results were neither what the company expected nor what it wanted. The company wanted a weak and poorly positioned operation to be turned around immediately into a profitable one. Joe did that."

But the company also wanted and expected much more. The company expected the immediate turn around to be the first step in a long and steady increase in profitability ending in industry leadership. This, of course, was utterly unrealistic.

In fact, there was no way for any of these businesses to be converted into long-term profitable leaders without substantial long-term investment which would necessarily be very heavy in the beginning. The risk would have been high. The end result would have been completely dependent on the established leaders already in place as competitors.

The company had no strategy and confused short-term operating goals with long-term investment decisions and investment evaluation. Neither Joe nor the company knew what they were really doing or what they should have done.

A Requiem for Joe

His company wanted the impossible and
expected Joe to get it.

Joe gave his company what they asked for
but not what they expected.

Poor Joe, he did the right thing for the
wrong reason and was fired for the wrong
thing for the wrong reason.

PROFIT CENTER ETHICS

Profit center managers are frequently caught in a cruel dilemma when asked to carry out policies that they strongly feel to be unwise. Yet they know that they will be held responsible for failure, whatever the cause.

The ethics of dissent are a very real issue in profit center management. Is the good of the corporation the overriding concern? Or is it personal survival? How far should dissent be pushed if higher authority neither wants nor accepts advice? What is honorable when either protest or acquiescence leads to unacceptable consequences?

The situation is real even with the best of good will on all sides. Differences in perspective lead to far different projections of consequences. Clearcut orders can be followed and must be followed. But orders to a profit center are rarely clear-cut just because it is a profit center.

By definition, a profit center is measured on results. In theory, future profit is the measure, and the manager is free to follow his own judgment within specific constraints. In theory, current performance is factored by the long-term benefits and the effect of corporate constraints. In fact, none of these conditions are ever wholly true.

Characteristically, the performance of profit center managers is measured over a moderate time span. The penalty for unsatisfactory absolute performance over the short-term is severe. But the proper balance between known performance and potential future benefits is never clear.

Executive stress is difficult to overstate when there is conflict among policy restrictions, near-term performance, long-term good of the company, and personal survival.

Logically, a profit center should have a combination of all kinds of goals simultaneously. The management should be judged on the net results of this complex of goals. Yet if this is done, profit is merely a derivative of the interactions of the various goals and constraints over time. It is not a prime index of current performance. It would not be the conventional profit center if it were managed this way.

The manager's situation becomes more difficult when members of the corporate staff are deeply involved. Should the manager do what is politically expedient and satisfy the preferences of staff advisors or optimize future performance for which he is held accountable? This can be an excruciating choice.

Corporate staff individually and collectively have their own ideas of how the business should be run. They are in a position to press those ideas hard. They can also significantly bias the evaluation of performance and the imposition of constraints. Failure to obtain their full support means being judged rigidly, even harshly, on near-term results. Yet the disagreement almost always concerns the longer term consequences. *The most important decisions a manager makes tend to depress short-term reported performance in order to improve long-term results significantly.* The issue becomes "should I do what is expedient, or should I fulfill my responsibilities to the best of my ability?" Martyrs are rarely honored in business.

In most corporations the evaluation of the profit center manager is based on current reported profit. Managers know it. Incentive compensation schemes often tend to reinforce this specific measurement over all others.

The problems of ethics are inherently chronic. The manager's problem can be serious enough even in the absence of any constraints. The temptation is great to take the performance measurement at stated face value. It is all too easy to liquidate the future and thereby maximize apparent current performance. In many cases this leads to promotion, leaving the aftermath to the hapless successor.

When the overall interests of the company impose constraints or goals that conflict with short-term profit performance, the conflict of interest is compounded. Both count; a balance must be struck. Compliance with the conflicting constraints and contribution to corporate goals are apt to be evaluated in a subjective and often uncertain fashion. Political expediency becomes a necessity.

The problem becomes even more acute when corporate management has a short-term time horizon and profit center optimization requires long-term investments of expense as well as capital. No manager who has a longer time horizon than his superiors can expect to survive. But neither can the business survive if the time horizon is inadequate to encompass the actions required today in order to protect the business in the future.

The worst of all situations exists when corporate management has a concept of the requirements for future success which differs from the profit center manager's concept. Such differences in perspective and philosophy can apply both to the profit center itself and to the corporation as a whole.

There are often tradeoffs between personal career and the good of the company. There can be real dilemmas where only short-term survival seems possible because of the tradeoffs between long-term and short-term performance. The conflict between expediency and responsibility can become painful. When any of these conditions exist, then managerial ethics becomes a real issue.

Regardless of ethics, everyone who aspires to responsibility in a complex organization must strike some balance. Those who are most realistic in their compromises inherit the responsibility and set the pattern for the future. That pattern may not represent the best interests of the company.

Resolution of this conflict can occur only if three conditions are met:

There must be an explicit corporate strategy. To be useful, the strategy must relate administrative behavior to the allocation of resources over time. Action must be seen in the context of a value system that all members of management understand and accept.

There must be an understanding and acceptance of the strategy on the part of everyone who is in a position to make decisions and tradeoffs that would affect implementation.

Appraisal of profit center performance must encompass a time horizon equal to the strategy time horizon.

Few multidivision corporations have a strategy that is adequate to spare their profit center managers the stress implicit in the ethics of dissent.

THE CHIEF AND HIS STAFF:
A Letter to the Chief Executive of a Multidivison Company

Dear George,

Our last discussion started me thinking about your organization problem. I came to two conclusions that are important enough for you to give them some thought.

First, you cannot expect to use your group vice presidents as your corporate staff. It cannot work. Second, you need and must have a strong staff reporting to you. I will explain my reasoning.

Your group executives are first of all line executives. As such, they are directly responsible for everything that happens in their groups. This requires a special relationship between them and the other group executives. In a complex company, the groups must cooperate with each other. Nothing would be more destructive to this cooperation than open criticism of another group vice president's policies in your presence.

As long as the group vice presidents have line responsibility, they will find it very difficult to discuss openly corporate-wide policies in your presence. After all, *every* operation is some group vice president's direct responsibility. This does not mean that group vice presidents will not have strong opinions and discuss them privately with each other. They will. It does mean they won't debate policy in front of you if there is any implied infringement on anyone else's operation.

As chief executive you must have an opportunity to hear your key lieutenants debate company affairs in your presence without any necessity for you to participate. You should be in the position of the judge in a law court who encourages argument in his presence but reserves judgment until he has heard the arguments.

This is why you need a strong corporate staff. Your corporate staff should provide the material and the arguments for discussion. The staff itself should be strong enough to be on at least an equal footing with the group vice presidents. Saying this another way: the corporate staff should have no fear or need of favor from anyone.

I suspect that you are finding the chief executive's spot to be a lonely one. You have a great deal of power, and it is a very weighty thing. Even your best friends find it difficult to argue with you or tell you that you are wrong — if they work for you. No one likes to tell you bad news. Your most casual wish is apt to be treated as a command. Ask any chief executive if this is not true. The nature of the chief executive's job shuts off free and easy communication with his peers. He has no peers anymore inside the company. The problem, of course, is to reconstruct a more formal communication system which will provide the necessary inputs.

Some chief executives run their affairs by having informal advisors who have great influence. One U.S. President, Tyler, I believe, had a group of cronies whom he depended upon so heavily they became known as the "kitchen cabinet." Others rely almost solely on financial reports.

In the long run, all effective chief executives find it necessary to formalize their information systems and make them accountable for what they supply and what they exclude. This is almost always done by means of a strong corporate staff.

A really powerful corporate staff has its own dangers. If controlled by a strong and ambitious man, it can make the chief executive a prisoner of his information. When this happens, the chief of staff becomes the "Prime Minister" and the chief executive becomes a figurehead, at least in part. If the role is divided, then coordination of corporate staff becomes a major problem.

The objective is to have a corporate staff which does the following things:
1. Identifies key policy questions of major significance wherever they may be in the corporate affairs.
2. Researches these issues until all of the related facts have been organized in an orderly form.
3. Presents the results of its business research in such a form that all of the arguments on both sides of an issue are objectively stated and supported.
4. Clearly identifies the alternatives in such a fashion that they can be discussed and choices made.
5. After discussion and decision, provides the detailed "completed staff work" required to convert the decision into a set of instructions and programs in the name of the chief executive.

You should work the corporate staff to its limit night and day. Put the pressure on. Demand analyses, briefings, surveys, evaluations, studies, recommendations, alternate programs. Demand tightly reasoned, well-documented, expertly presented reports.

Such presentations should be made to you and all of your key officers as a deliberative body. Your role should be that of the judge. Encourage argument. Encourage debate. If necessary, provoke it. If necessary, push every person present to take a position on the presentation and then defend it. Use these presentations and the debate to force your key executives to keep you informed and make their own attitudes and knowledge clear. Reserve your own decision until you want to make it. You are the final arbitrator. But get the evidence out in the open.

This technique is as old as business and government. There are many variations. The DuPont and Standard Oil of New Jersey full time inside Board is one. In this version there is no one judge, but a panel of them. In this situation the key is that these directors have no staff and no duties except to be a director.

The military have other versions. McNamara had a personal evaluation staff which he used to decide what questions to ask the military and which full-fledged studies to request.

However, in any case, I think you should realize that development of fully adequate personal and corporate staff is the very foundation of good management in a major complex business.

Sincerely,

Bruce D. Henderson

THE FALLACY OF DECENTRALIZED ORGANIZATION

In recent years there has been a great deal of discussion of participation management. Doug McGregor's Theory X and Theory Y have become familiar to most businessmen. The behavioral scientists have accumulated impressive evidence that authority does in fact come from below, not above. Reference to "consent of the governed" is deep in the American tradition. Rothlisberger and Dickson demonstrated the dramatic effects of participation behavior at Hawthorne Works nearly forty years ago. Chester Barnard stated the theory of authority in elegantly precise language in *The Functions of the Executive*.

The disquieting fact is that the theory of profit centers and decentralized management does not seem to coincide with the way that the real world actually behaves. The problem is real enough and the decentralization solution appears to be the only practical one for any situations. Yet it seems obvious that there is a major gap between existing management philosophy and organizational form on one hand, and our observations about the requirements for effective group coordination and performance on the other.

In fact, it is a matter of common observation that the informal organization is vastly different from the formal organization. It is also a truism that an institution is effective unless its informal organization is well established. Many institutions are quite effective, even though they seem to break all the rules of organizational structure — universities, for example. Japanese companies can be extremely effective competitors even though their internal structure seems incomprehensible to the Westerner.

What really happens in a decentralized company with multiple profit centers is quite different from the idealized descriptions. This is as it should be. If the individual profit centers were completely independent, there would be no reason for the parent company to exist except as the custodian of a nonliquid investment portfolio.

Clearly, all large-scale organizations have the same problem. They are too large for all decisions to be centralized, yet decentralization can never be complete where there is any mutual dependence or similar relationship. Activities which affect each other must be coordinated.

This coordination is achieved in all organizations by means of policies. Most of these policies are informal and unwritten. They work through the informal organization more than they do through the formal organization. Their character closely resembles a culture or a tradition. These are the behavioral patterns that set the style and distinctive personality characteristics of every successful organization.

Such characteristic patterns are both a major element of strength and an obstacle to progress. They are a source of strength because they provide dependability and consistency of behavior without overloading the communications system. They are also a source of weakness since they resist any change or adaptation.

The greater the apparent decentralization, the more the profit center policies will tend to be independent and unresponsive to the parent company unless objectives and constraints are made formal and explicit.

It is a paradox that the greater the decentralization, the greater the need for both leadership and explicit policies from the top management. Leadership is the effective use of the informal organization to communicate objectives and approved means. Explicit policies free the decentralized organization to take the initiative safely within those policy constraints. Without explicit policies, the central organization cannot optimize the company as a whole or coordinate its parts. Or, it can mean that the decision making outside the central organization is paralyzed.

Informal policy formulation and review become less adequate as the organization grows larger and more complex. Effective decentralized organization requires an explicit strategy and statement of policy as its foundation. This policy must come from the top,

although formulation of the policy may be the result of the participation of many people — in fact should be the result of a general
acceptance by most of those who are important to the policy implementation.

The essential element, in any case, is an understanding of and
consensus on the organization's goals and the means for attaining
them. The consensus can come from directives or from wide participation. The understanding can come before or after the choice of
objectives has been made. The communication can take place
through leadership, the grapevine, repetition, or detailed instruction.
Eventually, the organization will develop unwritten policies and
implement them based upon the corporate strategy *as members of
the organization understand it.*

This will happen whether the organization is decentralized or
not. If the organization is in fact an organization, there is no such
thing as complete decentralization. There is only specialization of
decision making, coordination, and communication.

All the practical and basic organizational forms for complex
operations have certain common characteristics:

> centralized policy direction based on explicit strategy con-
> cepts
>
> decentralized operation administration of operations based
> on complex, not simple, operating standards and goals
>
> A quality of leadership which achieves consensus on both
> strategy implementation and operating standards

Profit centers and decentralization are oversimplified descriptions of this set of organizational relationships.

GROWTH AND CORPORATE STAFF

Multidivision businesses inhibit creativity and entrepreneural
behavior. The inhibition is inherent in the required organization.

A multidivision management exercises control over the divisions. It sets objectives, establishes constraints, evaluates performance, and compensates management. This control requires a
detailed understanding of the business, plus current facts. Corporate
staff provide this background and analysis.

The division manager faces a major dilemma. He must explain and sell the corporate staff on every major move that he makes. Yet the time and energy required are directly subtracted from that which can be devoted to the business itself. Lack of full support leads to disaster on complex or major efforts.

No divisional manager can justify an investment in the future that is not fully appreciated in the present. It is not enough to be right. Higher management must be aware of that rightness now. The corporate staff is the analytical and communication link.

In stable, slow-growth businesses, this line-staff arrangement works well. Performance can be measured in the present by financial criteria. Past policies have been proven successful. Rapid change or experimentation would introduce unnecessary risk. Corporate management has long experience in understanding the business.

In the stable, slow-growth business, no successful manager is likely to move faster than he can persuade, educate, and win support from corporate staff. Normally, it is not important that he should.

The rapid-growth business cannot prosper in this environment. Too many acts are investments in the future. Payout and performance cannot be measured relative to current financial criteria. The confusion and lack of polish inherent in rapid growth are invitations to criticism. The stress on management is necessarily great. Diversion of time and effort to staff and corporate liaison is proportionately far more costly to the small business. The choice of policy tradeoffs is more intuitive and harder to explain. Often, the successful policies are impossible to prove right in a convincing fashion in advance. The payouts, no matter how great, are often realized after a considerable time lag.

This is why most successful diversified companies tend to be made up of relatively stable, slow-growth businesses. This is also the reason why most successful conglomerates have almost no staff.

Staff is necessary for corporate management to be informed. Yet corporate staff can inhibit all the qualities of imagination, initiative, and creativity that are so necessary for growth and innovation. The best management of a multidivision business is like Thomas Jefferson's description of the best government: the best management manages least, in the operational sense.

This does not reduce the importance of the corporate management function. At the corporate level, the best management of the multidivision business is master of the art of strategy evaluation — with the least possible staff.

WITHOUT MERGERS

If no mergers were permitted, there would still be conglomerates. Diversification does not require merger. It merely requires the ability and willingness to invest in order to diversify. There are other consequences of mergers besides diversification.

Without mergers growing firms must always be self-financed, either by retained earnings or from the public capital market's appreciation of their worth. If their profits are not in proportion to their growth potential, then growth and development must usually be restrained to match their financial means.

Without mergers old and fading firms must always die. There is no other way to use their organization and to redirect the cash flow from their uneconomic and depreciating resources.

In a static economy mergers are not very significant. It is an observable fact that mergers increase when the economy is growing and decrease during periods of depressed business growth. This occurs because merger and acquisition is essentially an investment process. The opportunity for investment, as well as the need for funds, is at a maximum when growth is at a maximum. Fundamentally, a conglomerate is a grouping of businesses with a common source of capital and common financial management. It has credit based upon the company performance overall, not the individual businesses. It can concentrate its investment funds internally where the returns are the greatest.

The concentration of investment is almost always the most potentially rewarding in activities which are growing rapidly. These are often the very activities which require far more cash than they can generate. Conversely, the mature and well-established business area is rarely the one in which profits can be reinvested with the hope of more than moderate returns.

Experience curve theory says that in a high-growth product the initial price should be set low and kept low, even below cost, until approximately 50 percent or more of the total market has been obtained. Thereafter, prices should be held constant or decreased as required to maintain that market share. This usually means a constant price until the required market share is obtained, and then declining price in parallel with ever-declining costs (in constant dollars).

This optimum pattern, according to experience curve theory, produces the highest return on investment. It also provides the lowest price to the consumer and the most efficient and productive use of assets. Thus, both the consumer and the investor are major beneficiaries of this strategy. However, major or even massive investment is required to optimize costs, use of assets, and return on investment.

Only a firm with diversified products or businesses can optimize the development of a growth product with internal financing. A new growth product requires a large initial investment to accelerate market development, establish market share, provide facilities, develop organization, reduce costs, and insure leadership. The payoffs for success can be so high that only an uninformed competitor would be unwilling to accept equivalent current losses in exchange for the high return later. But this kind of investment is practical only for a diversified firm.

Tax laws favor internally generated funds. Expenses which are investments in the future are in fact joint investments by the company and the government. The tax effect is to cause the government to provide funds by tax credits which are directly in proportion to the tax on the eventual profits. This occurs only if other operations of the company are providing profits against which these expenses can be offset. Such other operations must be part of the same corporate entity for tax purposes, however. If dividends are involved, the tax attrition of investment funds is compounded. Only the diversified firm can treat the government as a co-investor. For all others, taxes are apt to be a direct burden on reinvestment.

The diversified firm is better equipped than the nondiversified company to survive and serve the consumer in a competitive growth economy. Because it can direct internal investment accurately to the most productive applications, the diversified firm can grow faster, sell for lower prices, be more profitable, and pay less for its capital.

Mergers accelerate the efficient use of corporate resources. If there were no mergers, diversified firms would still grow into conglomerates of the Litton and GE type. It would take longer for the efficient firms to displace the inefficient. The growth in GNP would not be so great, although the pattern of business would eventually be the same.

If there were no mergers, the loser would be the consumer and the national economy.

CONGLOMERATES IN THE FUTURE

Conglomerates are the normal and natural business form for efficiently channeling investment into the most productive use. If nature takes it course, then conglomerates will become the dominant form of business organization, particularly in the U.S.

This conclusion may seem surprising in view of the widespread criticism of the whole idea of a conglomerate. People do not seem to take conglomerates seriously as an effective form of business organization. Closed-end mutual funds, which are a very dilute form of conglomerate, nearly always sell at a deep discount. Apparently, even the antitrust division of the Justice Department does not take conglomerates very seriously as an effective competitor.

In a sense, almost all companies are conglomerates if they have more than a single product. The term "conglomerate," however, seems to be reserved for companies which have such diverse business interests that they are essentially independent except for their financial resources.

There is no difficulty in identifying Litton or Ling-Temco-Vaught as conglomerates. Textron is no longer so obviously composed of unrelated businesses. But General Electric is surely a conglomerate. Dupont, with only a limited interplay between its textile fibers and its automobile finishes, is also a conglomerate.

There is an infinite range of relatedness and, therefore, characteristics of a conglomerate. However, all true conglomerates, as distinct from holding companies of any kind, have one major characteristic in common. They are able to control the internal allocation of financial resources. As a corollary, every conglomerate has the ability to obtain financial resources, which is a function of the firm as a whole rather than of the individual parts. This particular characteristic is of critical importance.

The conglomerate is able to carry the process of business evolution to a higher level of complexity. Instead of developing a family of products, it is able to develop a family of businesses. Every product goes through a sequence in which first, it is a drain on corporate resources, then it becomes profitable but is still a cash drain because of the reinvestment required, and, finally, it generates excess cash. This process is obscured in most businesses because of the overlap between products in different stages of development. The smooth growth of a business may conceal the birth, development, growth, and maturity of a long and complex series of products. Within a business the products are usually closely related.

But businesses as a whole go through the same cycle. They tend to be unprofitable when very new, profitable but undercapitalized when their growth is the fastest, and then generators of cash when they become successful, mature, and slow in growth. The problems change with maturity. The young, fast-growth business needs capital to take advantage of its potential growth and exploit its opportunity. The mature business has problems finding suitable investments for its cash flow.

The conglomerate is exceedingly well positioned to discharge the function of directing capital investment into the most productive areas. It can be far more efficient and effective than the public capital market is ever likely to be.

The top management of even a far-flung and diverse company is better equipped than an outside investor to appraise the potential and characteristics of a growing business. Such a company has staff research capability and access to data that even the most detailed prospectus cannot provide to the general public.

This ability to divert and reinvest the cash flows of a mature business is very important. There is no reason to reinvest the profits of a business in further expansion of the same business merely because it has been successful in the past. General Motors is not the only successful company which would find it unwise or difficult to expand faster than its industry.

The U.S. tax structure characteristically severely curtails investment funds available for reinvestment, first, if they appear as reported profits and, again, if they pass through the hands of shareholders as dividends. As a consequence, any corporate form which permits reinvestment expenditures to be treated as an expense instead of capitalized has a major advantage. This attrition of investable capital is the effect of a company paying a normal income tax and the stockholder paying taxes on dividends received before the funds are reinvested. The value of this advantage is not small. Income taxes will take away about half the reinvestable funds if the cash flow is reported as a profit. If paid out in dividends before reinvestment, then only a fraction of this is left for reinvestment.

Any company which can treat its investments in growing businesses as an expense to be offset against other profit has a great advantage in terms of its cost of capital. Also, any company which can obtain its equity from internally generated funds has a far lower effective cost of capital than if it obtained those funds outside from stockholders, who can retain only a fraction of the proceeds they eventually receive in dividends.

The conglomerate is in an unexcelled position to obtain capital at the lowest possible cost and to put it to the best possible use. The question, of course, is: will it do so?

If conglomerates treat each of their divisions or units as separate and independent businesses, they fail to take advantage of their own strength. Traditional profit center management is a fatal defect in a conglomerate, since it concentrates attention on near-term reported earnings rather than investment potential. This is why most successful conglomerates have been composed of mature businesses and have been notably inconspicuous for their success in incubating new businesses. Conglomerates must behave like investors, not operators, if they are to realize their great potential.

Experience curve theory dramatizes how great the potential really is for a conglomerate. This theory states that costs are a direct function of accumulated market share. Furthermore, it states that investment in market share can have extremely high returns during the rapid growth phases of a product. As long as the growth rate exceeds the cost of capital, every year in the future is worth more in present value than the current year. Today's losses, therefore, may be very high-return investments, even if prices never go up, provided those losses protect or increase market share. If market share correlates with cost differential, then it can be translated into investment value.

If experience curve theory is correct, the logical consequence of competition will be extremely low prices initially on new products. These prices will tend to be so low as to be pre-emptive. They will also be stable. The net result will be very large negative cash flows for a considerable period until costs decline to match the low price. This will be followed by even larger positive cash flows as costs continue their decline and volume continues to increase. This pattern is already visible in certain kinds of military procurement and in the pricing of commercial aircraft. Prices never go up, but costs do continue to go down, thus producing the return on investment.

The conglomerate is eminently well suited to this kind of "expense investment." In fact, only a conglomerate can hold a portfolio of risks. Only the conglomerate can match positive and negative cash flows. Only the conglomerate can pair off the tax consequences of "expense investment." Only the conglomerate can accumulate and analyze the detailed information required to make a wise investment involving such massive initial negative cash flows.

Everything favors the conglomerate: tax laws, capital costs, sources of funds, breadth of business opportunity. This does not mean that conglomerates will automatically succeed. Their inherent advantage lies in their flexibility and many conglomerates are conspicuously lacking in flexibility. If the flexibility is not used, they are under a handicap. The individual business is given no advantage except uncertain financial backing. The corporate overhead structure can be a real burden if the conglomerate is managed as if each business were an independent and irreversible investment. There are quite a few lackluster conglomerates.

If the conglomerate is to realize its potential, it must have an investment and strategy development skill which goes well beyond the characteristic pattern of the independent business. Certainly, some corporations are going to do this. Those that do are quite likely to be the pre-eminent and dominant firms of the future.

III

COMPETITION AND CORPORATE MANAGEMENT

3

THE MINIMUM PROFIT

The minimum profit for survival is not zero. In a healthy economy, the required minimum profit is typically quite substantial. The average American company needs about 10 to 15 percent return before taxes on shareholder equity in order to survive. The return needs to be twice that if half the earnings are paid in dividends.

Failure to achieve a minimum profit means that growth in parallel with competitors cannot be self-financed and maintained, even with all earnings retained. Failure to achieve parity in growth means loss of market share. This, in turn, leads to an unfavorable shift in relative cost. The progressive deterioration of competitive position must eventually lead to a permanent negative cash flow.

Many products that show a reported profit are still net users of cash. It is probable that a majority of all products that report profits are permanent cash drains. Rarely does a firm have a significant positive cash flow unless it has a leading market share. There are more followers in every product than there are leaders.

Growth is normal in a healthy economy. In addition, inflation requires financial growth even in the absence of physical growth. This growth must be financed. Financing is required for the increase in both working capital and fixed assets. The minimum reported profit must be adequate to provide this either directly or by supplying the base for debt.

In every case, the shareholders' equity must eventually grow as fast as the business. There is no alternative. Any growth in value of equity per share requires an equivalent minimum profit margin on equity.

This minimum applies to the company as a whole, not to individual products. Consequently, competition means competitor versus competitor, not product versus product.

If there is a difference in profit margin between competitors, then the high-cost competitor must still earn a minimum profit to keep up. The low-cost competitor needs no more to keep up. The differential in cost is reflected in cash throwoff available for dividends or investment in other businesses.

A sales price which provides less than the minimum profit for any company will cause a shift in market share towards the competitor which already has the lowest cost.

The low-cost competitors have the option. They can buy market share by setting the price level so that competitors cannot earn the minimum profit and thereby finance their continued growth. However, their own cash throwoff in the future will be determined by the difference between their own cost and the minimum required profit of the highest cost survivor.

The minimum profit is a key reference in a critical strategy choice: which is more valuable — a larger market share at a lower cost and a lower price, or the status quo?

THE RULE OF THREE AND FOUR

A stable competitive market never has more than three significant competitors, the largest of which has no more than four times the market share of the smallest.

There are two conditions which create this rule:

A ratio of 2 to 1 in market share between any two competitors seems to be the equilibrium point at which it is neither practical nor advantageous for either competitor to increase or decrease share. This is an empirical observation.

Any competitor with less than one-quarter the share of the largest competitor cannot be an effective competitor. This, too, is empirical, but is predictable from experience curve relationships.

Characteristically, these conditions eventually lead to a market-share ranking of each competitor one-half that of the next largest competitor, with the smallest no less than one-quarter the largest. Mathematically, it is impossible to meet both conditions with more than three competitors.

The Rule of Three and Four is a hypothesis. It is not subject to rigorous proof. It does seem to match well the observable facts in fields as diverse as steam turbines, automobiles, baby food, soft drinks, and airplanes. If even approximately true, the implications are important.

The underlying logic is straightforward: cost is a function of market share as a result of the experience curve effect.

If two competitors have nearly equal shares, the one which increases relative share gains both volume and cost differential. The potential gain is high compared to the cost. For the leader, the opportunity diminishes as the share difference increases. A price reduction costs more and the potential gain is less. The 2-to-1 limit is approximate, but it seems to fit.

Yet when any two competitors actively compete, the most probable casualty is likely to be the weakest competitor in the arena. That, logically and typically, is the low-share competitor.

The limiting share ratio of 4 to 1 is also approximate, but seems to fit. If it is exceeded, then the probable cost differential produces very large profits for the leader and break-even prices for the low-share competitor. That differential, predicted by the experience curve, is enough to discourage further reinvestment and efforts to compete by the low-share competitor, unless the leader is willing to lose share by holding a price umbrella.

There are two exceptions to this result: a low-share competitor can achieve a leadership position in a given market sector and dominate it in terms of cost if (1) there is enough shared experience between that sector and the rest of the market, and the firm is a leader in the rest of the market; or (2) an otherwise prosperous company is willing for some reason to add continually more investment to a marginal minor product. This can be caused by accounting averaging, full line policy, or mismanagement.

Whatever the reason, it appears that the Rule of Three and Four is a good prediction of the results of effective competition.

There are many strategy implications:

> If there are large numbers of competitors, a shakeout is nearly inevitable in the absence of some external constraint or control on competition.

All competitors wishing to survive will have to grow faster than the market in order even to maintain their relative market shares with fewer competitors.

The eventual losers will have increasingly large negative cash flows if they try to grow at all.

All except the two largest share competitors either will be losers, and eventually eliminated, or will be marginal cash traps reporting profits periodically and reinvesting forever.

Less than a 30 percent share of the relevant market, or less than half the share of the leader, is a high-risk position if maintained.

The quicker an investment is cashed out or a market position, second only to the leader, is gained, then the lower the risk and the higher the probable return on investment.

Definition of the relevant market and its boundaries becomes a major strategy evaluation.

Knowledge of and familiarity with the investment policies and market share attitudes of the market leader are very important since these policies control the rate of the inevitable shakeout.

Shifts in market share at equivalent prices for equivalent products depend upon the relative willingness of each competitor to invest at rates higher than the sum of physical market growth and inflation rate. Any company unwilling to do so loses share. If all competitors are willing to do so, then prices and margins will be forced down by overcapacity until a competitor stops investing.

There are tactical implications which are equally important:

If the low-cost leader holds the price too high, the shakeout will be postponed, but that firm will lose market share until it is no longer the leader.

The faster the industry growth, the faster the shakeout occurs.

Near equality in share of the two market leaders tends to produce a shakeout of all other firms unless they jointly try to maintain the price level and lose share together.

The price/experience curve is an excellent indicator of whether the shakeout has started. If the price curve slope is 90 percent or flatter, the leader is probably losing share and still holding up the price. If the curve has a sharp break from 90 percent or above to 80 percent or less, then the shakeout will continue until the Rule of Three and Four is satisfied.

The market leader controls the initiative. If that company prices to hold share, there is no way to displace it unless it runs out of the money required to maintain its capacity share. However, many market leaders unwittingly sell off market share to maintain short-term operating profit.

A challenger expecting to displace an entrenched leader must do so indirectly, by capturing independent sectors, or be prepared to invest far more than the leader will need to invest to defend itself.

There are also public policy implications:

The lowest possible price will occur if there is only one competitor, provided that monopoly achieves full cost potential, even without competition, and passes it on to the customer.

The next lowest potential price to the customer is with two competitors, one of which has one-third and the other two-thirds of the market. Then cost and price will probably be about 5 percent higher than the monopoly would require.

The most probable, and perhaps the optimal relationship will exist when there are three competitors, and the largest has no more than 60 percent of the market and the smallest no less than 15 percent.

A rigorous application of the Rule of Three and Four would require identification of discrete, homogeneous market sectors in which all competitors are congruent in their competition. More typically, areas of competition overlap but are not identical. The barriers between sectors are sometimes surmountable, particularly if there are joint-cost elements with scale effects. Yet it is a commonly observable fact that most companies have only two or three significant competitors on any product which is producing a net positive cash flow. Other competitors are unimportant factors.

The Rule of Three and Four is not easy to apply. It depends on an accurate definition of relevant market. It requires many years to reach equilibrium unless the leader chooses to hold its share during the high-growth phase of product life. However, the rule appears to be inexorable.

If the Rule of Three and Four is inexorable, then common sense says: if you cannot be a leader in a product market sector, cash out as soon as practical. Take your writeoff. Take your tax loss. Take your cash value. Reinvest in products and markets where you can be a successful leader. Concentrate.

MARKET SHARE

Market share is very valuable. In a competitive business it determines relative profitability. If it does not seem to do so, it is nearly always because the relevant product market sector is misdefined or the leader is mismanaged.

But the market share must be defined in relation to the share of the leader. Absolute share is almost meaningless, except as an indicator of market stability and competitive maturity.

The leader has a lower cost than his competitors because his superior market share permits the accumulation of more experience. Relative market share and relative accumulated experience become effectively the same over time.

The least effective competitor determines the profit level for everyone else, including the leader. The high cost competitor must generate enough cash to hold his market share and finance himself. If he does not or cannot, then he drops out, and a more effective, lower cost competitor replaces him as the marginal competitor.

The profitability of the market leader is determined by the same price level that determines the profit of even the least effective competitor.

Effective competition between any head to head competitors tends to eliminate the high-cost competitor. When competitive market share is unstable, the high-cost competitor is constantly being eliminated. All those firms which will survive are gaining market share as marginal competitors drop out.

When market share is shifting, profitability is an extremely poor indicator of performance. It costs money to gain market share. That cost can rarely be capitalized. Gaining market share depresses earnings. Yet gaining market share is the only way to be among the two or three survivors of true competition.

Generally accepted accounting principles almost invariably cause market share liquidation of a business to show an increase in profits until the business can no longer compete at all. These accounting principles almost always cause market share increases to depress reported profits. The eventual consequence in terms of present value may be the opposite.

Typically, competition eventually reduces the number of effective competitors to three or less. Typically, the market share of each is twice that of the next smaller competitor (the Rule of Three and Four).

If this does not happen, it may be because the leader is maximizing short-term profit by selling off market share as a result of a price umbrella. Or it may be because the marginal competitor and all others choose not to grow even though they have an adequate return on the added investment. It may be that the apparent failure to compete is a misperception or misdefinition of the market sector that is relevant.

Market share definition must explicitly recognize the boundaries between competitors' capabilities. If any shift in market definition produces a potential cost differential between competitors, it is a relevant barrier between competitors. The importance of the boundary can be great or small. And since there are multiple boundaries that are partially interdependent, the definition of the relevant market is a complex matter.

The most important single question about market share is: "Market share of exactly what market?" It is not a relevant market unless it includes all the competitors which have an inherent cost advantage over others in any subsector of that market.

Ability to maintain a basic cost differential in a market sector provides the opportunity to gain a differential growth rate and a differential market share in that sector. This leads to an even greater differential advantage in cost. This advantage can be compounded until it becomes an advantage of such proportions that quite adequate profits can be earned, even though competitors can barely finance the maintenance of their own shares.

The fundamental rules of market share are these:

Define the market in a way in which you have the greatest
inherent cost differential advantage.

Incur only the costs which *that sector* is willing to pay for.

Concentrate your efforts on obtaining a leading share in *that
sector* with the potential cost advantage that leadership
offers.

Redefine the markets in adjacent sectors which share experience and cost with the sector in which you are a leader.
Repeat the process with these adjacent sectors.

The basic rule is concentrate where you can be a leader.

To be passive is to be defeated.
                                    — **Charles de Gaulle**

COMPETITION AND PROFITS

Profits are the reward for doing a better job.

Growth in market share is the reward for giving the customer
more for his money.

Yet giving the customer more for his money subtracts directly
from potential current profit. Any growth is an investment. But any
growth in market share is an added voluntary choice to forego
present income in order to benefit even more in the future. Is it a
good investment?

More market share enables you to do a better job. It provides
the opportunity for lower costs, with the resulting margins multiplied by higher volumes. Yet it takes time to change, even if competitors will stand still and let you. It requires more assets to serve
a large customer group. Market share increase is an investment with
a high but uncertain return, as well as a substantial but uncertain
risk.

Even if market share is a good investment, it must be financed
with limited funds. Rare is the company that has more money than
it can invest to advantage internally. Market share for one strategic
sector must be bought by sacrificing others.

It is a common observation that companies generally make most of their profits from a very small portion of their total product market. Examination usually demonstrates that an even smaller portion of the total business is generating virtually all of the net cash flow that finances other products, pays the overhead, pays the interest on debt, and pays the dividend. In fact, few companies could grow at all if they did not consist of a portfolio of business investments, some of which generate cash and some of which are large users of cash.

Managing this portfolio is the basic action of an ongoing strategy. The portfolio as a whole has intrinsic value and is the base for the ability to raise capital. Every internal investment and disinvestment changes that base. Usually, the fullest practical use of external capital sources is essential to a successful strategy. The portfolio must be managed as a unit in addition to the management of each part.

Within a company portfolio of products and businesses, there is an infinite choice of rates of investment, amounts of investment, and degrees of concentration. There are an equal number of choices concerning disinvestment. Yet all of these tradeoffs must be made with the cash flow balance of the total portfolio as the frame of reference.

Competitors are the most important variable of all. They are uncontrollable, although often predictable. Each strategic sector has its own competitor. And each of these competitors faces the same decisions, the same tradeoffs, and the same constraints as you do.

There is no reason why the relationship between competitors should be stable. There is every reason why the market shares of any two competitors should be quite unstable. Market share stability is the result of a competitor's mistake, or it is the result of artificial restraints on competition, such as antitrust limits on size, share, or growth.

The competitor with the largest market share should have a natural cost advantage. Increasing the market share should increase both the cost advantage and the cash flow to finance even faster growth. The natural consequence is increased concentration by each competitor in only those strategic sectors in which it can be a leader. Concentration is only possible by withdrawing from those sectors in which leadership and clear-cut superiority seem unattainable. Such concentration benefits everyone.

It is obvious that many business policies are not based on fact or logic but on intuitive convictions. Many of your own decisions can be analyzed with more rigor. But those of your foremost competitor will still be based on a forecast of his intuition.

Most reasonably successful companies are remarkably skillful and competent in their day-to-day operations. Their skills are high. Their knowledge is great. This competence is attested to by the great difficulty that a new entrant encounters in achieving equivalent skills, even with unlimited capital and dedication.

But many of the greatest companies, in terms of past success, are mediocre in their perception of strategy. They cling much too long to policies and concepts that brought them their past success.

Nothing in a business career provides experience that will teach strategy. The time horizon is too long, and the opportunities to learn from experience are too few. The very skills that lead to executive leadership often have little to do with the ability to conceive and evaluate strategy.

Real strategy decisions are basic, nearly irreversible, and have major long-term consequences. Strategy can lead to great success; lack of it will surely result in undifferentiated mediocrity. Unfortunately, successful strategy often requires actions directly opposed to short-term reported profit. In fact, most short-term optimization is self-defeating in the long term.

This is why the opportunity is so great.

THE EFFECTIVE COMPETITOR

The effective competitor is low in cost. The effective competitor converts his lower cost into lower prices for the customer. When he does, he drives out all competition. He can hardly avoid it if he is an effective competitor.

Two competitors rarely have equal costs. If would be mismanagement or a coincidence if they did. Differences in market share convert into differences in experience. Differences in accumulated experience convert directly into differences in cost in well managed organizatons. The competitor with the largest market share should always be the most effective competitor.

The larger the differences in market share, then the larger the differences in cost should become. If competition is effective, market share is unstable. Those who have the most should get more.

The competitor with the lowest cost must inevitably drive any other competitor out if both use the same debt and dividend policies.

Each company will grow at the same rate as its return on assets if neither uses interest-bearing debt nor pays a dividend. The company with the lowest cost will grow the fastest under these conditions.

If two competitors use the same debt-to-equity ratio and pay no dividend, then the low-cost competitor's growth rate will be leveraged even more than his competition. Debt helps the low cost competitor the most. Debt is also safest for the low-cost competitor. Equal use of debt accelerates the displacement of the higher cost competitor. Japanese industry is a good example of the process.

If both competitors retain the same percentage of earnings, then their *relative* growth rate is unaffected. Dividends slow growth, but equal dividend payouts provide equal handicaps.

Unfortunately and unwisely, the lowest cost competitor typically has the least debt and the highest dividend payout. By these policies he permits higher cost competition to grow faster. Eventually, this leads to competitors' costs being lower and his own becoming higher than they would or should be. The consumer and the economy are major losers by this failure to compete.

Prices would be forced down if all competitors used the same debt equity ratio and paid the same dividends in proportion to earnings. There would be no alternative.

If the sum of all competitors' growth exceeded the growth of the market itself, then prices would necessarily be forced down until the growth in capacity matched growth in market. If the low-cost competitor always had a proprotionately larger growth rate, then the high-cost competitors would always grow slower than the market.

If low-cost competitors grow faster than the market, then, conversely, high-cost competitors must grow slower. The experience curve effect accelerates the process. Costs will improve in proportion to growth rate, and the cost differential will widen at an accelerating rate. The net effect is still to drive out the high-cost competitor.

This process has occurred many times, but it has rarely been carried to its logical conclusion. Companies such as Eastman Kodak, IBM, and GM are examples. The antitrust laws have inhibited competition in the U.S. In Great Britain it has been company policy only. Many companies mistakenly choose profit margin now, instead of increased return on shareholders' equity later. However, within each multiproduct company there are many illustrations with specific products.

Almost every company makes most of its profit and generates all of its net cash for dividends from very few products. Almost invariably, these are products in which the company is substantially larger than its next largest competitor. Where this does not seem to be so, it is usually because the relevant market segment is not recognized. It would be very strange were this not true. If high market share results in low costs, then this is the inevitable result. Profit for the leader is not monopoly; it is efficiency. Of course, large margin times large size results in a large proportion of corporate income.

These behavioral and cost patterns are matters of fact. They are observable over and over in everyday affairs, once recognized.

Yet if these things are true, the free enterprise system is not working properly. Business is following policies which are not to its own benefit. Consumers are suffering from lack of competition. Antitrust laws are contraproductive. Conventional economic wisdom is silent on the real issues.

Free enterprise should result in the efficient displacing the less efficient. The consumer should be the beneficiary. But this is happening only to a limited extent.

Businesses that are the most efficient should grow faster than average. Actually many, if not most, of the low-cost competitors steadily lose market share because of their own efforts to optimize current profit margins instead of return on shareholders' investment.

Consumers are being forced to pay prices high enough to support the growth of high-cost competitors. Antitrust laws encourage this tax on consumers to support high-cost competition.

Conventional economics has very little to say about competitive equilibrium in a growth economy. It has virtually nothing to say about competition in an environment characterized by continual inflation, where financial growth is a prerequisite to survival. Worst of all, conventional economics ignores the fact that costs do decline forever in real terms. If this were not so, then growth in overall productivity would cease. The experience curve effect can be observed in any factory, any retailer, and any product which is subject to competition. Conventional economics is silent on the issues that count.

The effective competitor in a free enterprise system must inevitably approach a near monopoly in the given market-product segment. Yet the monopolist company may well fail to reduce costs as it could if competition were a cost reference. In the absence of effective competition, some kind of restraint on the monopolist is clearly essential for the public good.

Suppressing competition with antitrust laws which punish the consumer to protect the small and inefficient competitor is a particularly awkward and costly form of government regulation. If competition is restrained, then neither the high-cost nor the low-cost competitor will be as cost effective as it might be.

Encouraging full competition must, however, lead to concentration in near monopolies. This calls for another kind of government regulation. Most businessmen fear this with good reason. Bureaucrats and politicians have demonstrated the probable consequences in their management of cities and their treatment of regulated industries.

The concepts of private property and free enterprise are based on the assumption of a system of vigorous competition. If effective competition is unstable and requires that competition always lead to monopoly, then we must rethink our concepts of government's relation to free enterprise.

It is patently untrue that multiple small competitors can be as cost effective as concentrated competition. Consequently, efficient competition must lead to concentration.

The imposition of peacetime pay and price controls is a warning that free enterprise and competition have been found wanting. Controls would lead to shortages immediately or be unworkable without rationing if free enterprise competition were effective.

We have an ambiguity in our business economic thinking. This has led to a dichotomy in our business and national economic objectives. This must be resolved. It will be sooner or later. We may move toward the state socialism of Russia. The Russian economy has been socially stable, but it has proved an economic failure, and has sacrificed civil liberties and personal dignity. We may move toward the Japanese pattern of concentrated business and govern-ment-business partnership. Clearly, Japan now has the most efficient, effective, and healthy economy and society on earth.

We are not what we think we are. We do not have genuine competition. Instead, we have massive regulation. If we had real competition, we would have no labor monopolies, and we would have concentration of industry. Our situation is unstable in both fact and theory. We must change.

Meanwhile, individual businesses can greatly benefit themselves, their customers, and their shareholders by engaging in more sys-tematic competitiveness.

Most companies have large numbers of products or market segments that are cash traps. They may show a profit, but they will require additional cash input forever. Effective competition would liquidate their misery and save everyone unnecessary costs.

Many companies have fast-growth products which they cherish because of their growth. Most of these will be major drains on their companies' shareholders. If only market leaders have low costs, then most others will be costly failures. The rule for the growth product is simple: be a clear leader or get out. Anything else leads to wasted resources. Effective competition conserves resources and lowers costs.

Every successful company has some product-market segments in which it is a clear leader. The risk is low and the competitive cost differential is large. Effective competition would lead to replace-ment of shareholders' equity in these with debt and redeployment of the released resources into other competitive arenas.

The effective competitor is good for its shareholders. The ef-fective competitor is good for the consumer. The effective com-petitor is good for society. The effective competitor becomes a partner with government in the evolution and implementation of national policy.

You can always easily identify an effective competitor. It is the firm with the lowest cost, and it is gaining market share at a proportionate rate.

---

* It is obvious that the antitrust laws are the most serious of all obstacles to competition. It is equally obvious that some other form of regulation will be necessary as activity be-comes concentrated. In fact, sweeping regulation already exists in almost every corporate policy area. A government-business partnership may be a prerequisite to a stable society in the future. Only a near monopolist can have the margin of safety required to sacrifice competitive position in order to pay social dividends in the name of "corporate responsi-bility."

INEFFECTIVE COMPETITION

We have a society and an economy built on the concept of free enterprise regulated by competition. That concept starts with certain assumptions:

The efficient will displace the inefficient.

Competition will cause the benefits of low cost to be passed on to the consumer.

New investments of resources will be made where they are the most productive.

The basic underlying assumption, of course, is that the low-cost competitor can and will set a price that higher cost competitors cannot justify. If that happens, then all the other assumptions are validated.

On the other hand, if high-cost competitors gain market share, then all the other assumptions are invalid. We must then re-examine all of our ideas about free enterprise. Either we make free enterprise work, or we find an entirely different way of allocating resources.

We can observe that free enterprise is not working. We see that prices are often raised, although excess capacity exists. We see high-cost competition not only adding capacity, but often growing faster than lower cost competitors.

Our economy is far from free. Large sectors are regulated in detail. This is particularly true of power, communications, and transportation. Certain policy aspects are regulated or prohibited. This is particularly true of labor, prices, and finance. The tax structure significantly dampens certain economic effects and amplifies others. The administration and court interpretation of certain laws have a profoundly inhibiting effect on competitive behavior, especially the laws dealing with labor relations.

But disregarding the external obstacles to competition, why do businessmen *choose* not to compete? Obviously, they feel it is to their advantage. Yet it can be demonstrated that shareholders, as well as the public, would benefit greatly from more effective competition.

Typically, business strives to maximize earnings per share by:

maximizing return on assets

maximizing profit margin on sales

maximizing sales volume and price level

None of these objectives relate directly to competition. Competition is merely the constraint. A policy decision by the low-cost producer to stabilize competition by self-restraint can invalidate the entire concept of free enterprise.

Competition is inherently unstable if the efficient competitor follows its own best interests. Failure of the low-cost competitor to gain market share steadily and consistently is a failure of management, as well as a failure to serve the public interest. Prices could be lower, profits per share could be higher, productivity could be higher, and business could be more stable in almost every area if competition were more effective.

The low-cost competitor serves its own interests and public policy best if it:

keeps prices low enough to inhibit competitors' growth

adds capacity as necessary to pre-empt industry growth

substitutes debt for equity as long as total costs are still significantly below competition

continues to invest in cost reduction as long as the net return on new investment exceeds interest costs

It is an observable fact that there is a direct correlation between market share and cost potential. The competitor with the largest market share should have the lowest cost. If this is not true, then the market has not been defined properly. The only alternate explanation is inadequate management. Therefore, lower cost should lead to greater market share which should lead to even lower costs and even greater market share.

The competitive relationship is inherently unstable. Effective competition must lead to concentration. Failure to do so is a failure of competition. Failure to do so is a failure of the whole concept of free enterprise. This concentration requires government-business policy coordination and cooperation. If this is achieved, then the result is greater productivity for everyone. Japan has demonstrated how effective and productive this kind of economy can be.

Public policy must recognize that different business policies are essential. If competition leads to concentration, it also leads to monopoly. Yet failure to concentrate is failure to compete, with many of the same consequences as monopoly but without the cost benefits of concentration. Public policy must encourage and guide concentration, not prohibit it.

Business can help itself by adopting policies that focus on competitive cost differentials and return on equity instead of on margin and return on assets. But real competition must be delayed until anticompetitive legislation and interpretation of antitrust policy are modified.

True prosperity requires efficient, prosperous business which is responsive to public policy. This is unlikely to develop in the present business-government adversary climate. We already have far too much concentration of government regulation centered in an enormous and clumsy bureaucracy. Yet business and government must coordinate tax, trade, price, financing, and labor policies at least.

We should disband the regulations and dissolve the bureaucracy. Instead, we need a small, tightly coordinated government policy planning group. Such a group should have great influence but not direct regulatory power. Its influence should be exercised through indirect financial policy regulation of corporate debt, dividend, and tax policies.

Business-government policy coordination can be far more effective if business is concentrated. Fragmented and dispersed business leadership cannot coordinate with an all-powerful, self-serving, gigantic government bureaucracy. Government control is the most inflexible, autocratic, inefficient, and unresponsive monopoly of all.

Some industrial nations have progressed far in the alliance between government and business to establish policy but decentralize management. Their growth in national productivity has reflected this. The Japanese have provided a classic model worth emulating.

The alternatives for the future appear to be obvious and in stark contrast.

We can restore business competition in the classic sense. This means changing many business price policies, internal control measures, and financial policies. It requires an effort to obtain more realistic trade legislation. It leads to concentration. Eventually, it results in a business-government policy coordination very similar to that between management and its board of directors.

The alternative is a steady drift toward close bureaucratic regulation by an all-encompassing and hostile army of functionaries who are a law unto themselves.

The business policies of the low-cost competitor will determine the eventual results and the kind of society we choose. Business can help itself and improve its own performance by focusing on displacing the ineffective competitor and concentrating business with the efficient competitor. The general public will be the major beneficiary. The constraints and hostility of government will be obstacles, but not barriers, to a more productive society.

COMPETITIVE CONSIDERATIONS

It is against all logic for high-cost competitors to displace low-cost competitors. But they often do. It seems unreasonable for high-cost competitors to sell at lower prices, grow faster, and use more debt than low-cost competition. But they often do. If they did not, the original leader would never be displaced.

Successful business strategy requires that the lowest cost competitor be persuaded indirectly to give up its market share, cost leadership, and profitability. This obvious loss to the leader may result from competitors' superior strategy. More often it is a misperception of his own best interests.

Since all strategy depends on competitors' behavior, a firm's strategy choices are based on forecasts of competitors' plans and their reactions to the firm's initiatives.

Some decisions, such as pricing, can have different consequences for two competitors with different market shares and different costs. This is true even if they are competing in the same market with the same products. A given price change can affect competitors differently. One competitor's margin, growth rate, and cash flow will be changed substantially more or less than the other competitor's. The effect of pricing depends upon product mix and competitors' financial policies. It is a potent competitive weapon for changing market share.

Low cost and high market share go together. The relationship can be expressed rather accurately by the experience curve:

Unit costs net of inflation decline 20 to 30 percent each time accumulated experience doubles.

Cost

Potential cost soon becomes a function of market share. Market share is very valuable if it produces lower cost in addition to higher volume. Superior market share and superior growth can lead to a superior cost position which permits profitable operations, even at prices where competitors can only break even and cannot finance their own growth. This cost position can also allow safe support of sufficient debt to replace the original capital and redeploy it; the inferior cost position of competition cannot support debt.

Cost reduction potential is calculable because it is a function of *shared* experience and previous experience. Added experience may be a large or a small proportion of *previous* experience. This ratio determines cost reduction potential.

Some cost elements share their experience with other products. This means that costs may change because of joint experience, too.

Price

Over time prices must inevitably parallel costs. When they do not, market shares are changing. For example, the price of an American product tends to stay up until the leader has lost a substantial share of the market. Then a break in price usually occurs, and it appears to go down steadily at a faster rate of decline than cost. This continues thereafter for long periods, until only a few competitors are left. The original leader is often replaced. The Japanese pattern of competition is quite different. Their prices do parallel costs. But Japanese margins are adequate to finance only the low-cost leader's growth.

Market share is necessarily unstable unless the price parallels the experience curve cost decline. If prices decline faster than costs, then margins shrink. Sooner or later a competitor is squeezed out. At the very least, investment stops in a losing venture. If the market is growing, surviving firms gain share. As they do, they improve their relative cost position. This provides incentives for them to invest more while putting even greater pressure on those firms which have reduced their investment rates.

Conversely, the end result of holding prices high while costs are declining is usually to produce market share instability. In the shifting of share that results, the initial leader always loses share and relative cost position. In the long term, market share stability is again achieved when only a few survive. Frequently, the former leader is displaced.

Segments

These effects are often obscured because they occur in market segments, rather than in the broader industry categories generally used to define businesses. There are many sharply differentiated segments in any one substantial business area. Each segment has different cost elements. Each cost element has its own experience base and therefore, its own characteristic response to added volume. Identification of segment boundaries relative to competitive cost differentials is a critical element in business strategy.

Concentration of effort and investment in segments that can be defended permits eventual redeployment of resources to other segments, where the process can be repeated. In this way, limited resources can be used to overtake competitors with both lower costs and more capital.

Cash Flow

Cash flow is necessary to growth and cost reduction. Concentration in appropriate segments leads to superior market share in those segments. Superior market share leads to wider relative margins. Wider margins lead to greater cash flow per unit of output than that of competitors. Market share and cash availability are thus mutually dependent variables.

Cash needs are a function of growth. Faster growth means faster investment. Gaining market share requires more cash — it costs money to buy market share. Some product markets need more cash than they can generate in order to succeed. Others generate more cash than they can profitably invest. The balancing of the cash flows within a product portfolio matrix is a necessity for a successful strategy.

Treating each product or administrative unit alike is certain to be self-defeating in a competitive sense. Such equal treatment destroys all the advantage of diversification and imposes all the handicaps of overhead and unnecessary constraint.

The Consequences

Most competitors do not realize their potential. There are few companies which cannot sell at lower prices forever, yet pay shareholders higher dividends forever.

This potential for superior performance is dynamic, not static. Accomplishment requires sequencing and timing a series of carefully coordinated choices. True competition does lead to fundamentally lower costs and more for the customers' money, as well as a better return for the investor.

However, true competition leads to concentration of market share in the effective competitor. This is not necessarily the competitor with the most resources and lowest cost at the present time. The final outcome depends upon competitive strategy.

Successful strategy for the stronger competitor leads to a lower cost position and greater relative market share. Successful strategy for the stronger competitor also leads to increased market share and lower costs, while discouraging further investment by the higher cost competitors.

Increases in the quality of life and in national productivity require the development and use of superior competitive strategy. It can be done.

FAILURE TO COMPETE

The dominant producer in every business should increase its market share steadily. Failure to do so is prima facie evidence of failure to compete.

Cost and market share are inversely related. The highest market share should produce the lowest cost as a result of the experience curve effect. At least part of that superior cost should be passed on to the customer in lower prices of better quality, which, in turn, should lead to faster growth of the leading competitor.

Failure to gain market share, even with superior costs, is failure to compete. It is also a failure to achieve even lower costs.

Competitors' market shares should be unstable. Low-cost competitors should displace higher cost competitors. Customers should share the benefits of lower cost with those suppliers which make it possible. Any failure to gain market share, even with lower cost, is self-evident restraint of trade.

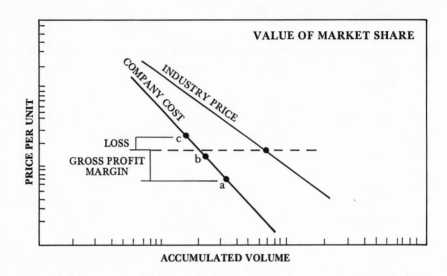

Displacement of high-cost competitors by lower prices benefits the customer. It leads to benign monopoly. No monopoly can be justly accused of exercising monopoly powers if it does not raise prices more than the extent of inflation.

Failure of an industry to concentrate is failure to compete and failure of the national economy to optimize productivity and reduce inflation.

INFLATION AND COMPETITION

The natural effect of inflation is to concentrate business in fewer hands, slow down growth, and shift the investment process from private to government control. If it continues for a long time at high levels, inflation eventually will tend to result in state-financed and managed industry, regardless of who the owners are.

These things happen because inflation changes the equilibrium of the competitive system in a growing economy with an income tax. All competitors are not affected equally by inflation. Producers with high debt will be endangered more than those with less debt. Low-margin producers will be affected more than high-margin pro-

---

* See your lawyer before gaining market share if you are a leader. What is best for the customer and the country is not necessarily legal.

ducers. Anything which interferes with prices outrunning inflation
in costs will result in an accelerated concentration of business in the
hands of the high-margin, low-debt companies.

The specific business consequences of inflation are almost
exactly the same as those that would be created by a major tax
increase. This is why inflation can easily produce a depressing reaction if not offset or controlled. This is in addition to the automatic
increase in tax rates on personal income as a result of a progressive
tax.

Inflation is the equivalent of a tax on all business assets — a
direct tax which occurs automatically, without regard to government
taxes. Every asset of a business which is not permanent must be
replaced eventually at an inflated price. Yet the higher replacement
cost does not represent an increase in value. The difference in original and replacement costs is a drain on the business. It must be
financed from retained earnings or borrowed money. This means
that prices of finished products in a growth industry must go up
faster than inflation in costs, or one of three things will happen:

Growth will slow down.

Debt ratios will increase.

Dividends will be cut.

Typically, the marginal producer is able to pay little if any
dividend and has limited debt capacity because of low profit margins.
This means that the marginal producer is hit first and hardest by
inflation. The marginal producer is forced to slow up or stop its
growth unless its prices go up faster than the inflation in its costs.
Since this rarely happens, the marginal producer tends to be
squeezed out and industry is concentrated in fewer hands.

Even those strong and profitable companies which can with-
stand the squeeze are faced with the same three alternatives. If the
industry growth continues, these firms must grow even faster to
compensate for the marginal firms which cannot finance their
growth. But inflation requires more debt to finance inflation, in
addition to financing real growth. Monetary controls to restrain
inflation may make added debt unavailable, particularly to the firm
which has already fully utilized its potential financial resources.
Even the prosperous firms are likely to find continued growth
difficult unless prices increase *faster* than costs.

Direct government taxes greatly exaggerate all of these effects:

All internal, nondebt financing must eventually come from
profit after taxes. In the U.S. this means that profits typically
must be twice as much as needed to finance growth. Faster
growth requires higher profit margins.

Inflation itself is a tax. Income taxes apply to the difference
between original cost and replacement cost, as well as to profits. The tax is on money value growth, not size or capacity.

Income taxes add a tax on inflation, too. All personal tax
rates are increased by inflation; in effect, all tax brackets are
lowered.

The net effect of inflation is to transfer a substantial part of the
flow of investable funds from private to government hands. This
can be good or bad, depending upon how wisely the government,
compared to private industry, invests these funds.

In the U.S., the federal government alone has a cash income
flow of nearly 22 percent of the GNP. State and local government
take a not inconsequential 12 percent. This does not include the
large segment of business in which government effectively applies
"administrative guidance" on operating policy and prices, as in rail-
roads, airlines, shipping, all communications, and all central station
power. All natural resources, including agriculture, are semiregulated
as well. A major portion of the flow of investment funds is already in
government hands. Inflation will increase this proportion.

Inflation will also increase business dependence on government.
Government controls the fiscal policies which produce or control
inflation. Government controls the monetary policies which determine the investable funds available to industry. Government controls
the tax policies which determine the impact of both fiscal and
monetary policies on the individual. Government controls the
administrative machinery which sets policy on prices, labor relations,
investment areas, product design, and many other critical decisions.

Inflation will increase the influence of government on business
development and evolution. And inflation seems to be here to stay,
as a natural corollary of prevailing public policies (full employment,
in particular). With continued inflation, it is becoming increasingly
clear that government and business are really part of the same economic and social system and must act and coordinate accordingly.

Businessmen cannot control inflation. If prices go up slower than costs, the least profitable firms cannot finance their growth in a growing economy. The result must inevitably be increased concentration in fewer producers. Of course, if continued for a long time, this would lend to shortages, just as price controls always do.

Concentration in the most efficient producer is not bad. In fact, it is necessary for minimum cost. However, the concentration of power in private hands will inevitably result in more government administrative control. Inflation will hasten the process.

There are several strategy implications of inflation. True profit margins will be squeezed in spite of higher reported profits. Cash requirements will be increased and so will the cost of money. These forces, of course, also lead to a concentration of industry and an increasing degree of interaction, in the area of policy, between government and business.

IV

INFLATION AND
CORPORATE MANAGEMENT

4
⚮

AMERICAN INFLATION AND POLITICS[1]

1946-1948: President Truman and the Republican Congress

It was pure luck. But everything was done exactly right. As a result, inflation, generated by a tripling of the money supply during World War II, was allowd to expire naturally in 1948.

> Truman pleaded with Congress to extend wartime price controls. Congress sent him such a weak bill that he vetoed it.
>
> In the next two years, neither money supply nor federal debt was increased at all. The latent inflation suppressed by wartime controls burst out and ran its course in about a year and a half. Prices increased about 50 percent, then stopped rising of their own accord when they regained equilibrium with the money supply.

The inflation was over. Truman had tried to retain controls. The Federal Reserve had tried to control interest rates, not money supply. No one knew what they were doing, but it happened to be the correct thing.

1950-1952: The Korean War

The Korean War did not result in a federal budget deficit. However, prices did at first rise sharply because money velocity

---

* Written in collaboration with Jens O. Parsson, author of *Dying of Money: Lessons of the Great German and American Inflations,* Wellspring Press, Boston, 1974.

increased rapidly as buyers tried to beat feared wartime shortages. If the government had been wise or lucky enough to do nothing, prices would have fallen all the way back when the scare buying subsided. The Federal Reserve tried to hold down interest rates by increasing the money supply 16 percent in the 1950-1952 period, so that prices rose 13 percent. We still did not know what we were doing.

1952-1962: The Eisenhower Years

This was the least inflationary ten-year period in the last 60 years. Money supply increased about 1 percent per year and prices did the same during this time.

However, average stability for that period included increasingly severe oscillations between boom and recession in a shorter and shorter cycle as the government tried to fine tune, and instead overcontrolled the money supply.

    1953-1954 — Stability
    1954-1956 — Expand
        1957 — Contract
    1958-1959 — Expand
        1960 — Contract
        1961 — Expand
        1962 — Contract

The stock market, business prosperity, and employment faithfully followed the change in money supply. Prices could not shift direction that fast and were, therefore, relatively stable. However, at the time of the 1960 election, the U.S. was economically stronger and sounder than at anytime before or since. Unfortunately, the 1960 downswing timing changed the political party in power to one willing to seek expansion at any price including unlimited inflation.

1962-1968: The Kennedy - Johnson Era

The Eisenhower policies were continued from Kennedy's election in 1960 until October 1962. In that month real inflation began. The monetary inflation proceeded at the rate of 4.6 percent per year — faster than at any time since World War II — for the first 43 months, through April 1966. There was a brief deflationary interlude in 1966, then from January 1967 through April 1969 the money supply grew at 7.2 percent per year for that 27-month period. The total added monetary inflation was about 38 percent by then and growing. Prices, lagging behind, had so far increased by only about 11 percent. The difference was latent inflation. This expansion of money and purchasing power faster than their value at first could fall made possible an unprecedented temporary prosperity.

During this period from 1960 to 1968, the total number of productive workers in all the fundamentally useful industries remained constant at 27 million. However, an incredibly large number of workers — 12 million — were added to the national payroll. Profit margins were lower in 1968, a boom year, than in 1960, a recession year. Workers in these basic industries fared no better. Real gains in hourly wages were lower in the boom of the 1960's than in the noninflationary Eisenhower years, and were declining. These were disastrous years of apparent prosperity under an administration whose economic philosophies embraced monetary inflation as a panacea. It was, as usual, effective temporarily.

The monetary inflation bought a phony boom. It also lit the fire under inflation and fanned it until Nixon was unfortunate enough to inherit the shambles by being elected President in 1968.

1968-1976: Republican Fire Fighting

Phase One (1968-1970). Efforts to balance the budget came first. For 1969 and 1970 combined, the federal budget showed a slight surplus. Meanwhile, the Federal Reserve slowed down the growth in money supply from around 8 percent in early 1968 to less than 4 percent in the spring of 1969. All central banks, the Federal Reserve included, tend to be responsive to the policies of the party in power, as they should and must.

Predictably, the stock market fell. In a little over a year, stock prices were down more than 30 percent. Interest rates reached new heights with the credit crunch. Slowly, business began to sour, profits plummeted, unemployment rose, and recession came.

Paying the piper for the 1962-1968 dance was extremely painful, and not enough had yet been paid. Prices continued to rise. The latent inflation had not yet been realized and equilibrium had not been reached. Money was still growing fast enough to perpetuate 3 or 4 percent inflation, even if the latent inflation had been squeezed out and equilibrium achieved. Worst of all, time was running out before the next presidential election.

By 1970 the 1972 election was clearly on the horizon. There is no way for a political party to deflate and to be elected simultaneously. The direction of the battle had to be reversed, temporarily at least. The retreat was into more inflation.

Commencing approximately in August 1970, the budget deficit reached a peacetime record. Money inflation shot up again to more than 8 percent. The stock market soared and prosperity returned. Interest rates fell. After a long wait, employment increased again and the recession ended.

Phase Two (1970-1972). Price increases had continued up at about a 4 percent, and the new boom would surely soon accelerate that rate. Price controls were clamped on on August 15, 1971. Prosperity was returning and liberals were being appeased. It was another dose of the narcotic. The pain would have to be faced again after the election.

Controls bottled up the still unpaid bill for the 1962-1968 inflation and postponed it with compound interest. About a 20 to 25 percent rise in prices to match the previous growth in money supply was still due. Yet money supply was compounding at a faster rate than ever before. Inflation forever was the prognosis if that trend continued. But economic sophistry and demagogic travesty won the 1972 presidential election for the Republicans by giving the nation a renewed boom for an election present. Promise them anything but get elected if you wish to have any future influence.

Phase Three (1972-1975). With the election over, boom and inflation had to be faced again. The artificially repressed prices of 1972, while masked under controls, had caused a breakneck boom and shortages, which further unbalanced and, therefore, increased inventories. By 1973 the nation's production capacity was strained to the limit.

At the beginning of 1973, two months after the election, price controls were removed. Prices again started to chase the money supply in search of equilibrium. Wholesale prices, which had increased only 6.5 percent in 1972, increased by more than 18 percent in both 1973 and 1974. This was double-digit inflation. Prices, once released from controls, burst out like the air from a toy balloon, until the latent inflation finally approached exhaustion.

Meanwhile, the money supply growth itself was steadily braked down from 9.2 percent in 1972, to 6 percent in 1973, to 4.7 percent in 1974. As long as prices were increasing so much faster than money supply, the latent inflation was being eliminated. It was just the reverse of the creation of latent inflation from 1962 to 1968. The bill for the 1962-1968 spree was still due, but now it was being paid in full. As soon as prices regained equilibrium with money supply, inflation would slow down by itself, just as it had done in 1948. This happened around the end of 1974, when money supply was about 90 percent larger than in 1962 and prices were about 80 percent higher. With the latent inflation finally eliminated, the increase of wholesale prices in 1975 was exactly equal to the increase of money supply at 4.2 percent.

Another part of the bill for the 1962-1968 spree was the worst depression in a generation. This, too, was the reverse of the creation of latent inflation. Real GNP output from 1973 to the end of 1974 dropped more than 6 percent, until it bottomed out at the end of 1974. The tight money ran up the yield on three-month Treasury bills from 4 percent in 1972 to 8 percent in 1974. The price-earnings ratio on common stocks went from over 18 in 1972 to under 9 in 1974. In fact, the stock market dropped almost 40 percent.

To its everlasting credit, the Federal Reserve did not return to rapid money supply expansion in the face of a barrage of Congressional demands and an election less than a year away. It held the line around 5 percent. Of course, that was not a low rate of money expansion by comparison with the Eisenhower years or even the early years of the Kennedy-Johnson inflation, but it was the lowest sustained rate of money expansion since 1966.

In spite of the Federal Reserve's tight hold on money expansion and the lack of fresh monetary stimulation, the depression bottomed out, almost as if on command, at the end of 1974. The stock market started a long climb back to near its all time high (in inflated dollars only, however). GNP in real terms moved up steadily from a low in the first quarter of 1975 and began to approach its previous all-time high. Total employment approached its all-time peak and passed it in early 1976. The inflationary fires were burning themselves out. The money supply was growing no faster than prices, yet real prosperity was returning fast.

Most of the medicine had been hard to take, but the patient, the national economy, was finally getting well again. However, 1976 — another presidential election year — was approaching. Would the economic prognosis be relapse, remission, or health? And after that?

Fateful 1976: Year of Decision

In 1949, 1953, and 1962 the United States achieved essential equilibrium between money supply and price level. The year 1976 may well be once more a year of near equilibrium and a chance to cage the inflationary tiger. The price has been paid for another chance of peace and prosperity, with inflation stabilized not at zero but at least at a moderate rate. The decision now is a political one. The problem is political, not economic.

Starting from monetary equilibrium, any healthy economy can buy a period of prosperity by constantly increasing the money supply faster than prices rise. Of course, prices will rise faster and faster following the money supply. This is what was done from 1962 through 1968 "to get the country moving."

A monetary holocaust lies at the end of that path. Germany in 1923 went all the way to complete destruction of its money. The memory still lives in Germany of that desperate time.

The temporary boom of inflation is not prosperity. But it is politically very, very seductive. Every really liberal politician implicitly promises that the road will be paved with good intentions and be very pleasant to walk down.

There is the possibility of starting down the garden path slowly and then retracing the steps after the next election and before the disaster. It can be done. The price is another depression plus inflation too. If the process goes very far and that next election is lost, then the opposition party is faced with a shambles and a nearly impossible task. At best, the opposition, if in power, will be faced with both inflation and depression simultaneously in their turn in office. That will not likely cause them to be reelected. Whoever is elected will be faced with either more austerity or eventual disaster.

Further recurrence of boom and bust with inflation can so disillusion the electorate that only that last resort to the authoritarian, self-perpetuating strong man seems possible. Those in office, whoever they are, may inherit that unlimited power.

There is also the alternative of the sober prosperity of the Eisenhower years with virtually no inflation. But that is not politically expedient. It may not be adequate to be either elected or re-elected.

No presidential election since the great depression of the 1930's has been so clearly and obviously focused on economic issues up until now (April 1976). And no political decision in 200 years has so much potential for changing the economic future of the United States of America if that remains the key issue until election time. Ominously, many candidates and dominant political elements promise to put heavy pressure on the Federal Reserve to raise the rate of money expansion, and with it the rate of inflation.

The irony may well be that the extraordinary economic insight of the Chairman of the Federal Reserve combined with the intestinal fortitude of the first President to resist liberal loose money expediency, will result in a wholly unforeseen combination of reasonable prosperity and tolerable inflation during an election year. If so, perhaps the goddess of luck still smiles upon us. Can she do so for another 200 years?

INFLATION IS:

Inflation is much more than rising prices. It is a struggle for a bigger share. It is the cost of absorbing a larger work force. It is the price for pollution control and part of the price for strikes and work restriction. It is part of the penalty for throttling a market economy with antitrust, tariffs, price controls, minimum wages, crop support, and balanced trade. It is also the advance payment required for a higher standard of living in the future. Yet little of this is true inflation. Apparent inflation is the price of intangibles or the present cost of a better future.

True inflation can be caused by excess government expenditure (fiscal policy) or by creation of excess credit (monetary policy). But much of a price increase is pseudoinflation. When the economy is near capacity, anything which diverts output will increase prices on the rest of the output. The price increase has all the effects of inflation. Yet the total output per capita has not changed. This diversion of output can be government spending, trade balance change, environmental expenditure, and even vital capital formation.

Many events can change the apparent cost of living, in terms of price level, as much as true inflation. Some expenditures are highly desirable to preserve the future. Others merely postpone consumption in order to compound future consumption.

Inflation does not change the real average standard of living in an economy at capacity. Prices may go up, but on average just as much is produced and sold per person. Inflation may redistribute income, yet it does not change the average. Anything which gives one person more current consumption in a full economy takes it from someone else.

The classic cure for inflation *can* increase the real cost of living by decreasing the total ouput available for consumption. That cure restricts the money supply until a depression of business stops the growth in prices. This recession reduces *real* output. On average, less is produced per person. Unfortunately, the reduction in buying power tends to be concentrated in those who become unemployed. The cure can be worse than the disease.

Increases in employment can appear to be inflation. An increase in total employment requires added capital. The average manufacturing employee in the U.S. requires about $25,000 in assets. The two million or more added employees in the U.S. each year requires $25,000 x 2,000,000, or more than $50 billion. This is equal to the average annual after-tax profits of *all* U.S. corporations over the last ten years. Work performed to produce these assets must be paid for. But this work produces no consumer goods. It merely allows the new employee to be as productive as the average employee was before the new employee was added. Someone must defer current consumption to make this possible. An increase in prices is required to depress the demand of others to make room for the new employees.

Environmental improvement shows up as inflation. Pollution control is worth the cost. If this were not true, why would we voluntarily inflict the cost on ourselves? The cost is significant. In the U.S., starting around 1968, energy consumption increased about 6 to 7 percent compared to GNP. Energy consumption is a good index of cost incurred. Therefore, pollution control added about 7 percent to the cost of everything else. Pollution control is not inflation. But it raises prices and reduces output of other benefits in exchange for environmental benefits that are not measured in the consumer price index.

An improved trade balance shows up as inflation. A change from an unfavorable to a favorable balance of trade raises prices and reduces consumption. An excess of exports requires that you produce more than you consume. If the economy has been at capacity, then the shift in trade balance is in fact a shift in level of consumption. Changes in price level are merely a means of rationing the available output among consumers. The increase in prices due to increased exports appears to be inflation, but it is not.

Controls cause real inflation. Controls always lower total output. Employment is distorted. Use of facilities is distorted. Shortages are created. Shortages increase inventories because the shortages cause mismatching of other components. If the total consumer output is reduced, then the average standard of living must be lowered either by shortages or higher prices.

Strikes or work stoppages of any kind generate real inflation by reducing the output available for consumption. Work stoppages have far-reaching effects in a modern economy. People's lives are disrupted and productivity is destroyed in many interrelated activities. If increased prices are used to spread the loss, this constitutes real, self-inflicted inflation.

Reduced foreign trade is real inflation because it decreases total output. All trade is based on obtaining something in return of greater value than the value of that which is sold. Foreign trade therefore increases the effective supplies obtainable with available employment and capacity. Reduction in foreign trade is reduction in real value of employment.

Future improvement in living standards feels like inflation now. Higher standards of living require increased productivity, which requires added capital investment per capita. Increased investment requires decreased consumption until the increased investment pays off in more output.

Prices have increased. By definition, price increases are called inflation. But large parts of the price increases are the result of our own choice. We need more price increases now (capital formation) to hold down prices later.

We should call investment in the future something besides "inflation." A different term should be used to describe investment in environmental control, trade balance redress, population growth employment, and the expenses of increased government. We should recognize that the drive behind real inflation is often an escalation of the struggle for a bigger share of a limited economy.

However we describe inflation, we can have no more than the total that we produce. Inflation is simply an involuntary division of our common output, call it what you will.

INFLATION AND THE CORPORATE PLANNER

Inflation may appear to be bullish to the stock market; it is anything but helpful to the corporation. It means an acute shortage of funds which can choke off growth even though it may stiffen demand. It means earnings which will be reported and taxed but which will never be available for growth or dividends. Even the higher prices for end products are not necessarily helpful when materials and labor costs go up at least as much.

The price effects on inflation receive much more attention than the critical effect on cash needs. When all prices go up, the asset side of the balance sheet must go up in proportion. Except for certain permanent assets, such as land, each item must be increased in proportion to the change in price levels. This means that otherwise identical assets must be purchased at higher cost to do the same task that previously could be performed with lower valued assets.

The difference between the original cost and the later cost represents an outlay of cash. This cash had to come from somewhere. It can come from debt or from retained earnings. Either way, there are problems.

If cash comes from retained earnings, it means that taxes have been paid on that income, causing a cash drain, yet the earnings must be permanently reinvested in the business. In effect, the inflation was really a loss, although half of it was reported as a net profit.

If the cash comes from debt, then it constitutes a claim that comes before those of stockholders. Therefore, the debt required because of inflation is in fact a straight deduction from previously reported earnings.

It is not easy to obtain debt to deal with inflation. Creditors want net returns which are still net after offsetting the effects of inflation on the value of money. This means that interest rates become high. Furthermore, no one wants to make long-term loans if there is any likelihood of rates of inflation increasing. Long-term money gets expensive. Also, since everyone needs money at the same time for the same reason, it may become hard to get it at all.

The effects differ for different kinds of companies. Companies with rapid capital turnover are hardly affected. Very small increases in prices completely offset the effects of inflation on capital required. Capital-intensive industries are not affected at first unless they try to grow. But with time, capital-intensive industries must develop profit margins equal to the inflation rate times the capital turnover rate, just to avoid increasing their debt ratio.

Public utilities, chemical manufacturers, computer leasers, and heavy machinery producers are particularly hard hit. For them, inflation requires very high rates of reported income just to have anything left beyond that required merely to sustain the business.

Growth industries with slow capital turnover are apt to find severe constraints on their growth. It may be impossible to increase profit margins enough to provide the capital for growth, provide the capital to offset inflation, and pay taxes on the reported profit which this would make necessary. As a consequence, many growth companies are severely hurt by inflation.

For any company, dividend payout merely multiplies the effect of inflation. Dividends tend to be a casualty if the company is growing and has a substantial capital-to-sales ratio.

Ordinarily, many capital-intensive companies are able to compete effectively at reasonable margins on sales just because they have high debt levels. Inflation can drastically curtail the growth of these companies if debt isn't available to maintain their debt ratio. At a time when they must raise added capital just to stand still, they are forced to reduce their debt-equity ratio and supply the added capital for inflation from retained earnings. This may make growth impossible.

The visible effect of inflation is to raise prices. Prices would not rise, however, if supply and demand stayed in balance. Competition would insure that. Prices do rise primarily because suppliers *cannot* grow as fast as demand without higher prices to supply their cash needs. In other words, inflation chokes off growth in physical volume, even though apparent dollar volume may increase.

It is clear that growth in reported profits during inflationary periods is not translated into benefits to stockholders, or even to employees. In addition, however, the effect on competition and corporate strategy can be equally critical.

In the capital-intensive industry, the company which is growing and already has a high debt-equity ratio obviously faces a formidable obstacle. Conversely, the company with a debt-equity ratio in the same industry has an unusual opportunity to steal a disproportionate share of the growth, if willing creditors can be found.

Growth companies face extremely severe problems if their physical capacity expansion means equivalent expansion in their capital investment. After all, a growth rate of 10 percent annually means the equivalent of doubling capacity by the seventh year. The effect of inflation is likely to shift the competition between growth companies from operating efficiency toward financial resources.

One thing is sure: inflation of a substantial amount introduces a major added variable into corporate strategy. Certain companies face considerable handicaps in their competitive performance. Others are in an improved position to gain on competition.

Strategies to obtain a competitive advantage from inflation are peculiarly difficult to formulate, however. It is not easy for the strategist to remember that net cash flows are all that count. Inflation often makes a large part of reported earnings unavailable for either growth or dividends — ever.

LIVING WITH INFLATION

Inflation will be with us for a while. Business policies required to survive and succeed during periods of inflation are not the customary ones. Margins must be proportionately higher and prices must go up faster than inflation. Inflation of the balance sheet must be financed. The increase in the net assets must come from retained after-tax profits or increasing ratios of debt.

The real cost of debt is decreased by inflation. Real interest rates after discounting for inflation will often be negative. Failure to use the maximum safe debt is very dangerous during an inflationary period in a competitive industry. The competitor using the most debt with negative real interest has a large advantage.

Yet use of debt is potentially dangerous during inflationary periods. Periodic liquidity crunches are almost a certainty as attempts are made to wring the inflation out of the economy. The first rule is to avoid catastrophe: be certain that you can roll your debt over as necessary.

Inflation causes financial growth to become the sum of inflation rate *plus* the rate of physical growth. Even physically slow-growing businesses become fast-growth businesses financially. Fast growth compresses the time required for competitive actions and reactions to take place. Price policies and capital investment plans must be judged accordingly.

Marginal producers will be squeezed out by inflation. Without inflation, marginal competitors grow under the price umbrella of lower cost competitors which use little debt and pay high dividends while the marginal competitors do the opposite. When the financial growth required by inflation forces leaders to use debt, while inflation reduces the credit standing of weaker competitors, then the permissible profit margin differential narrows. Inflation reduces the difference between successful survivors and competitive drop-outs.

The business cycle is exaggerated by inflation. Low-interest rates, prosperity, and physical growth are characteristically followed in due time by exponentially increasing inflation. Otherwise, prosperity will be followed by continued inflation plus high-interest rates, with at least mild depression. There is no quick relief from inflation once it is firmly embedded in the economy.

Efforts to impose controls do not usually last long because they do not work very well. But they produce severe distortions in the economy while in effect. During controls, marginal products become severe liabilities. They require increasing infusions of cash at the very time that they adversely affect credit worthiness during a period of rationed credit. All kinds of shortages, in addition to cash, are inevitable and predictable if controls are continued for long. Controls will force larger than normal inventories because of the shortages.

The effect of inflation is to produce boom conditions while the inflation rate is increasing. As long as this condition lasts, unemployment will be low, and interest rates will be modest compared to those of future inflation rates. However, for this situation to continue, the rate of increase in future inflation must be exponential. This situation is obviously limited by time because it leads inevitably to a breakdown of the value of money. Cessation of the rate of increase in inflation will lead to sustained inflation, but without prosperity.

A real reduction of embedded inflation is almost always preceded by a long period of depressed business, unemployment, high interest rates, and liquidity constraints.

Inflation and the business conditions required to reduce it are equally sensitive political issues. It is predictable that national policies with respect to inflation will tend to oscillate between extremes once it becomes a political issue. The full effects of changes in monetary policy, controls, and business behavior tend to lag well behind the actions themselves. As a consequence, there is a strong tendency toward over-control and over-reaction.

Business and national policy can fully adapt to any steady state of inflation. It is a change in the rate of inflation that produces most of the problems and side effects. The effect of inflation is nearly negligible if all decisions about money commitments are made with reference to a known, constant, and assured rate of inflation. Under these conditions, inflation continued over a long period of time is a nuisance, but not a problem. However, inflation has not been steady, nor will it be in the foreseeable future.

The prospect for the predictable future is substantial inflation, with rates varying widely from year to year. This will be coupled with periodic liquidity squeezes. Alternating periods of boom and depression are to be expected. These conditions are both a threat and an opportunity for enterprises engaged in competitive business.

THE END OF INFLATION

Businessmen can be patriots and end inflation by raising prices. Of course, no one will think they are patriotic. Conversely, businessmen can appear patriotic and statesmanlike while being extremely aggressive and even predatory in holding prices down. In fact, business can benefit everyone, including the consumer, by raising prices to end inflation or holding them down to eliminate the higher cost producers.

Inflation will end when prices go up more than wages and other forms of personal income. Paradoxical as this seems, it cannot be otherwise. The popular definition of inflation is "rising prices." However, this is only the visible symptom. More precisely, inflation is an instability between prices and costs which accelerates the increase in costs. The only way to stop cost increases and restore stable equilibrium is to increase prices *faster* than costs or to increase capacity, which takes time.

The instability occurs when demand exceeds supply — both of which are normally regulated by price. An increase in price should reduce demand and eventually increase supply. Anything that prevents a price rise or full use of existing capacity automatically interferes with the ability of the economy to be self-adjusting and stable. Anything that interferes with the addition of capacity and the increase in output automatically interferes with the ability of the economy to stop inflation and resume normal growth.

Price increases must outstrip cost increases until available capacity outstrips demand, otherwise inflation not only never ends but constantly accelerates.

That is why the end of a period of inflation is always accompanied by rising prices without a corresponding increase in personal income.

It is also why, in the aftermath of inflation, available capacity finally outstrips ability to buy.

These facts of life do not mean that an individual business will profit most by raising prices, even though it can do so and make them stick. All competitors do not suffer or benefit equally from a change in price levels. Certain competitors can gain a great deal by maintaining constant prices. The profit they forego is returned with substantial compound interest far into the future. Market growth, compounded by growth in share, compounded by lower relative costs, compounded by increased safe leverage, can produce profits in the future that amply repay foregone profits now.

A period of inflation is a particularly opportune time to change market share, especially if the government is using monetary policy to fight inflation. There is ample evidence that market shares rarely change unless capacity is inadequate for some reason. Periods of inflation are characterized by almost full capacity utilization. Furthermore, tight credit restricts the addition of new capacity.

Major increases in capital expenditures during a period of inflation are not only good economics, but also good business for all except high-cost producers. Since only low-cost producers can get the added capital for capacity expansion during a period of monetary restriction, one of the effects of inflation should be to shift market share to the hands of the most efficient producers. But this must be done by holding down prices to inhibit the growth of the less efficient.

Price is the critical control of the competitive system. Very small differences in price can make major differences in the ability to grow or expand capacity. This sensitivity is not spread equally among competitors. Inflation is a period of opportunity for the low-cost producer. It is a period of greatly increased risk for the higher cost, lower margin producer.

Typically, the high-cost producer is highly leveraged, pays a small percentage of earnings in dividends, and has a small margin on sales. A slight price decrease can completely inhibit this producer's ability to raise the required money or take the inherent risks to increase capacity. Inflation squeezes the firm's profits and restricts its growth. A price rise in excess of inflation is the only means of salvation. The high-cost producer must not only match the cost increase with the increased revenues, but make enough extra to pay the income tax on the write-up in asset value which will occur with every asset turnover.

Conversely, the low-cost producer with wider margins, less leverage, and a dividend as a cushion can not only raise the money to expand capacity but can well afford to take the risks and defer the benefits. By merely holding prices constant — which amounts to lowering prices during an inflationary period — and making certain that capacity is equal to all customer demands, the low-cost producer can increase market share and consequently decrease relative cost. This would be very difficult to achieve in any other period.

Inflation has all the financial consequences of growth that would occur with an increase in physical volume in an economy without inflation. However, inflation also produces an added restriction in monetary supply that compounds both the rewards and the penalties for the use of financial policies as a major component of corporate strategy.

A period of inflation is quite likely to bring some substantial shifts in competitive performance. Which firms benefit and prosper will depend upon who has the insights and takes the consequent actions. Some strategists will understand the feedbacks and sensitivities of the competitive system in a dynamic phase. Most will not.

THE RISK OF UNCONTROLLABLE INFLATION

Lessons from Germany
1921 to November 1923[1]

When the debacle finally stopped in 1923, the old German mark, which had once been worth a solid 23 U.S. cents, was worth

---

*Written in collaboration with Jens O. Parsson, author of *Dying of Money: Lessons of the Great German and American Inflations,* Wellspring Press, Boston, 1974.

one-trillionth of that. Money was worthless. It would buy nothing. All debts were effectively cancelled, all mortgages were paid off, all bank accounts were useless. Nothing could be bought or sold.

The whole German system ground to a halt. Factories closed. The middle class disappeared. Only barter was left. There were food riots and terrorism. Hitler's famous Putsch beer hall of November 1923 was only one of many, and not the worst.

How did it happen? It started when Germany did not pay adequately for the 1914-1918 war with taxes. Instead, the country covered its deficits with war loans and issues of new paper reichsmarks. Scarcely one-eighth of the wartime expenses had been covered by taxes.

After the war, Germany and all the other combatants underwent price inflations which served as partial corrections for their wartime financing practices. The year 1919 was a year of violent inflation in every country, including the United States. By the spring of 1920, German prices had reached 17 times their prewar level. From this point, however, the paths of Germany and the other nations diverged.

The other nations stopped their deficit financing and took their medicine in the form of an acute recession in 1920 and 1921. Their prices fell steeply from the 1920 level. But Germany continued to inflate. Prices in that country temporarily stabilized and remained rock steady during 15 months in 1920 and 1921. There was, therefore, no surface inflation at all. But the government had begun to pump out money at a renewed rate. Germany's money supply doubled once more during this period of stable prices.

The catastrophe of 1923 was begotten not in 1923, nor at any time after the inflation began to mount, but in the relatively good times of 1920 and 1921. Easy money spread; there was a boom. Industry and business were going at fever pitch, and great fortunes were made by "profiteers." Unemployment was nonexistent.

While many workers were able to keep up with inflation through union activity, many others fell into poverty. Salaried and white-collar workers lost ground. Regional separatism was so strong it came close to breaking Germany into fragments. The crime rate soared.

The ratio of office and administrative workers to production workers rose out of all control. Incessant labor disputes and collective bargaining consumed great amounts of time and effort. Whole industries of fringe activities and middlemen sprang up.

Almost any kind of business could make money. The boom had suspended the normal processes of natural selection. That was during the boom; afterward all of this activity vanished.

Inexorably, inflation had begun to stalk the boom. After holding steady for the 15 months preceding July 1921, prices doubled in the next four months and increased by ten times through the summer of 1922.

The government's actual deficits were relatively innocuous. The national budget was closer to balance at the brink of the crash in 1922 than at any time since 1914. But the inflation had become self-sustaining. The government was unable to refinance its existing debts except by printing new money.

The final convulsion, when it began, was at first bizarre; then it became a sheer nightmare. Beginning in July 1922, prices rose tenfold in four months, two-hundredfold in 11 months. Near the end, in 1923, prices were at least quadrupling every week. In the end, the total real value of all the reichsmarks in the world was smaller than it had ever been, a phenomenon which enabled the government's economists to argue that there was no true inflation at all, just numbers.

The new rentenmark, which was issued alongside the devalued reichsmark, carried no real value except the naked avowal that there would be only so many rentenmarks and no more. The Germans miraculously believed it, and still more miraculously, it turned out to be true.

The granddaddy of all credit squeezes followed Dr. Schacht's order of April 7, 1924, which stopped all credit from the Reichsbank. Inflation was finally halted.

Unemployment temporarily skyrocketed. Government spending was slashed, taxes raised, working hours increased, and wages cut. Almost 400,000 government workers alone were discharged. The shock to the German people of the final inflation, followed by unemployment, was so great that in the election of May 1924, six months after the end of inflation, millions of voters flocked from the moderate center parties to either the Communists or the Nazis on the extremes. These parties gained dramatic strength.

Germany very quickly began to feel better economically, however, as the stabilization medicine did its work. New elections only seven months later, in December 1924, repudiated the Nazis and Communists and restored the strength of the middle-class parties.

Schacht warned against relying on foreign loans, but was ignored. In fact, the revival was based, to a significant degree, on foreign loans. The world depression which followed 1929 knocked debtor Germany flat again, and Hitler followed close behind.

The expansion of Germany's money supply always led the way in the inflation. When the former abated temporarily, the latter did the same. When the money supply stopped permanently, inflation also stopped permanently.

What happened in Germany can happen anywhere. If the money supply grows faster than output of real goods and services, there will inevitably be an equivalent inflation sooner or later, usually after a lag and a temporary boom.

All politicians who wish to cure unemployment by an increase in money supply, please take notice. It can happen again.

THE MINIMUM INFLATION [1]

Five percent is now the minimum trend line inflation for the U.S. It will be that or more until the Federal Reserve sets 5 percent as a maximum annual growth rate of money supply. Inflation could be zero, but only if the growth of money supply were also near zero.

Ever since 1949, price inflation has averaged about one-half of one percent per year less than the expansion of the money supply (M_1). This held true not only over the entire 26 years, but also over each of the three cycles within that period from one point of equilibrium to the next.

AVERAGE ANNUAL INCREASE

	Money Supply	Wholesale Prices	Differences
1949 - 1953	4.2%	3.6%	0.6%
1953 - 1962	1.4	0.8	0.6
1962 - 1975	5.3	4.9	0.4

---

* Written in collaboration with Jens O. Parsson, author of *Dying of Money: Lessons of the Great German and American Inflations,* Wellspring Press, Boston, 1974.

The difference of only about one-half of one percent a year between money expansion and price inflation has been the same, whether the actual rates of increases have been high or low. This implies that one-half of one percent a year was all the money supply expansion that could be permitted without causing inflation. Any money expansion in excess of that was translated directly into price inflation sooner or later.

Now (August 1976) the prevailing rate of expansion of money supply is about 5 percent per year. Disregarding temporary fluctuations, the year-to-year rate of expansion has been in that vicinity since early 1975. As long as a rate of money expansion as high as 5 percent prevails and the constant relationship of the last 26 years between money and inflation holds, inflation, too, must average within a fraction of a point of 5 percent per year.

The 5-percent rate of money supply expansion, which thus appears to assure a 5-percent inflation rate, also appears to be the lowest rate of money expansion we can tolerate politically, because the fear of inflation is not enough to offset the politically seductive possibility of short-term prosperity. That rate of expansion represents the bottom end of the Federal Reserve's present target range, and no one is seriously proposing to reduce it further. The debate is focused on how much it should be increased to "reduce unemployment." Therefore, 5 percent a year now seems to be the accepted minimum rate of money expansion, and as long as new money pours out at that speed, it is an idle hope to suppose that price inflation can average less than the same 5 percent a year.

Money supply expansion at this rate is considerably more restrained than the very high rates of recent years, but it is by no means low. It is higher than the average of the inflationary Korean War years, close to four times the average of the Eisenhower years, and about the same as the overall average of the inflation cycle from 1962 to the present. It is probably the best we can do under the circumstances, but let no one suppose that it is noninflationary.

The reason why inflation is so nearly identical to money expansion, in spite of economic growth and the need for more money, is related to money velocity. The rate of use of money has steadily risen at roughly the same speed as real growth ever since World War II. That means that velocity increase alone has supplied all the additional purchasing power justified by real growth, and virtually no increased money quantity in addition could be absorbed without causing inflation. Velocity has been increasing faster than ever in recent years, and this may cause inflation to be even higher in relation to money supply expansion in the past.

The close identity between money supply and prices, of course, does not necessarily hold good at all times or in the short term, but only between points of equilibrium, such as 1949, 1953, 1962, and 1975. When money grows faster than prices, then the gap is latent inflation, to be released when money growth slows down. This happened from 1962 to 1968, when money supply increased faster than prices until the latent inflation was well over 20 percent by 1968. Equilibrium could not be achieved until prices caught up and closed the gap. Double-digit inflation finally did that. The inflation was not only predictable, it was predictable in amount. This equilibrium was accomplished by early 1975. When the gap had been closed, the previously inevitable double-digit inflation became very unlikely until the money supply growth rate accelerated again. We have reached another natural equilibrium.

The real question now is not whether inflation can be further reduced, but whether money expansion and price inflation can be held permanently as low as the 5-percent base rate. That rate of money expansion is not as high as in past recoveries. Heavy pressure on the Federal Reserve to raise the rate for better prosperity can be expected. A higher rate of money expansion undoubtedly would achieve a better prosperity, but at the price of inevitably high inflation. The dominant political forces in the nation which demand faster money expansion are, in effect, demanding a further increase in the base rate of price inflation.

Whether or not the Federal Reserve will be permitted to hold the 5-percent line is the pivotal economic issue before us. Twenty-six years of experience warn us that every percentage point more of money supply that the Federal Reserve is forced to provide will amount to just one point more of price inflation in the long run. Each time we increase money expansion one more notch to achieve a better prosperity, we take one step closer to triggering a runaway inflation cycle.

The evidence of history seems to show that the level or prosperity is independent of inflation as long as that inflation is stable and unchanging. If anything, steady-state inflation is a depressant of prosperity.

Increasing the money supply does buy a period of prosperity, but only as long as the *rate of increase* is increasing too. When this happens, prices lag behind money supply and latent inflation is stored up, even though the rate of inflation is growing.

When the rate of growth of money supply becomes constant, the lagging prices start to catch up and the latent inflation is released. Equilibrium can only be achieved eventually with parallel growth in money and inflation rates. But prices will keep on rising until cumulative growth in money supply has been matched by cumulative price increases.

Any decrease in money supply growth rate produces a depression and may cause even faster price increases if money velocity and production levels are affected. But eventually, price increases again will become parallel to growth in money, and there will be steady-state equilibrium.

There is no way to buy prosperity by increasing money supply, except on a temporary basis.

Increase in money supply is like an increase in dosage of a hard drug narcotic addict. It feels good at first. But it takes an increasing dosage just to feel normal. Withdrawal is extremely painful, but further increase is deadly.

The road to inflation is a politically seductive primrose path strewn with promises of full employment, prosperity, and plenty. But the end of the path is disaster. Yet turning back is politically lethal for whomever may seem to be responsible.

The choice between short-term prosperity and long-term inflation is a political decision made at the polls. The campaign oratory preceding elections reveals the subtle differences between hypocrisy, ignorance, and expediency on one hand, and insight, honesty, statesmanship, and leadership on the other.

INFLATION AND THE WORK ETHIC

The desire for a classless society with relatively moderate differences in standards of living top to bottom is an age-old aspiration of many cultures and nations. It has never been achieved, although it is closer now than ever before. The obstacle to achievement is fundamental. Improvement in the average standard of living requires an increase in capital intensiveness. This is another way of saying that wealth must be accumulated. But wealth is compounded when it is well used. Anything which prevents the compounding of wealth also prevents potential improvement in the quality of life.

This worldwide trend promises to level all incomes in each country. The usual method is to sharply graduate the income tax and then tax investment income even more heavily. Inflation accelerates the process, since progressive tax brackets are automatically lowered, thus making the tax heavier for any given level of real income.

The objectives of the individual therefore tend to focus on:

security of employment and income at the expense of level of income

certainty of job tenure and, ultimately, an adequate pension

minimum working time rather than maximum annual income

pleasure in work rather than increased direct rewards

These work patterns on balance favor government employment or very large business employment at the expense of other kinds. The trend favors the elimination of small business. Even very large businesses will undergo major changes in employee relations. Every failure to adjust will accelerate the trend toward government as the only employer.

Large-scale business will gradually be forced to substitute optional delayed retirement, increased pensions, job security, amenities, perquisites, and stability for the concept of "a fair wage for a fair day's work." Employment becomes a marriage contract, not an arm's length transaction. Only the very large and stable firm can provide any reasonable assurance of the essential long-term employment security. By comparison, the government becomes a more and more attractive employer.

Private business is always badly squeezed for capital when there is inflation. Inflation is financial growth and must be financed exactly like physical growth. Return on assets *after taxes* must at least equal inflation to avoid physical shrinkage. The alternative is an ever-increasing proportion of debt capital in an economy in which people are unable to save and are being discouraged from saving.

Private-sector debt must come from private savings. If saving is not rewarding, then very little saving will occur. Rising interest rates encourage saving in the absence of heavy taxes. But taxes plus inflation can make almost any interest rate unattractive. This, too, tends to make the government and the government alone able to raise capital.

The consequences are far-reaching. High progressive income taxes coupled with inflation virtually guarantee that most of the population will become wards of the state or alternately dependent on their employer's pension. Only a limited amount can be kept after taxes on original income. Even less can be retained after taxes on the earnings of savings. Less still remains after inflation depreciates the remainder. Self-financed retirement becomes almost an impossibility, except for the most fortunate and successful.

This pattern leads to a totalitarian state. It also leads to an ineffective economy characterized by low productivity. A different tax philosophy can achieve both an egalitarian society and a highly productive, mobile, and fast-growing economy.

This conflict among personal incentive, the need for capital formation, and the desire for a classless society can be reconciled. Tax policy is the tool. Long-term personal security and eventual leisure are the incentives if the tax structure is right. Personal savings and capital accumulation can be the mechanism for both insuring security and providing the future output to support it.

The impact of taxes should be to:

encourage savings by individuals

encourage debt utilization by corporations

limit the personal-expenditure rates of individuals without limiting their capital accumulation

The desire for a classless society should not be allowed to destroy the individual's ability to provide for his own security. Neither should social objectives be allowed to undermine the capital formation process that provides the whole foundation for a better life.

Our future social structure and quality of life depend on tax policy, yet the power to tax is the power to destroy. Capital formation must not be destroyed; personal saving must not be destroyed; and the work ethic must not be destroyed. Compounding of productive capital must be allowed. A classless society with ever-improving standards of living is possible, political restrictions permitting.

CONTROLS AND INFLATION

Inflation, unemployment, and depression often occur simultaneously; they should not. The cause is excessive control. This control is ever present in the form of thousands of regulations that interfere with normal responses to supply and demand. An end to inflation requires controls that reinforce supply and demand instead of blocking them.

True market prices will always go down as long as there are two competitors with unused capacity. Regulation often holds price up. Failure to compete actively does the same.

True market pay levels will always go down as long as no shortage of workers exists. Regulations, work laws, and union restrictions prevent these adjustments, even when willing and able unemployed job candidates are available.

Conversely, price and pay should, and do, go up with shortages. But they should go *both* up and down. Prices and pay that only go up are proof of a failure of competition and a breakdown of free enterprise.

If pay and prices do not respond quickly and sensitively to market forces, then the whole free enterprise concept is invalid. There are only two alternatives. Use controls to strengthen market response or use controls as a substitute for market response.

Any price increase in the absence of a shortage is *prima facie* evidence of market failure. Any group pay increase in the absence of a worker shortage is evidence of a labor market failure (monopoly). Any failure of pay levels to decline when there is a labor surplus is a market failure.

Full and effective competition inevitably tends to concentrate in the low-cost producer. Failure to concentrate is proof of the failure of a market economy. True concentration leads to the need to control a monopoly in the public interest. The end result of an effective competitive market can only be some kind of control.

Likewise, in an industrial society there are a multitude of work groups, each of which can hold the economy for ransom if it acts as a collective bargaining agency. If members of such groups act collectively, they are a monopoly. Effective collective bargaining can only end in anarchy or external control of collective actions.

An industrial society soon becomes subject to thousands of constraints, regulations, laws, and customs. Each could be worthy of praise for its goals. But collectively they paralyze the market place and its ability to match supply with demand. Simultaneous inflation, shortage, and unemployment are the result.

Normally, controls are not an antidote to regulation. They are more of the same thing that caused the problem. The minimum control is the best, because it allows prices to go down and productivity to rise. During America's greatest growth period, there was a steady decline of prices for nearly 30 years. This was in a virtually regulation-free society, however.

Controls can paralyze. Yet controls can produce personal freedom, stability, and prosperity. The good controls are those which make pay and price *more* responsive to market forces.

Controls which stabilize prices and pay lower the standard of living and cause inflation and unemployment. Only controls which cause price and pay to respond more *quickly* to supply and demand can eliminate the damage of inflation.

Three kinds of controls comprise the foundation for an inflation-free, full-employment, prosperous society. The first is control of the money supply in circulation. The second is control of obstacles to competition, leading to concentration and competition. The final control is policy coordination between business and government when the desired concentration is achieved. The alternative uses of control lead in the opposite direction.

V

PRICING AND MARKET SHARE

5

~~~

PRICE STRATEGY WITH INFLATION

Experience curve theory says that about 3 percent steady annual growth on trend in physical volume is required to reduce costs enough to offset 1 percent of annual inflation. Only products with growth rates more than three times inflation can expect to hold a constant price in current dollars without producing a shakeout.

There are some general pricing rules. Price parallel to experience curve costs if market shares are to be kept constant. Raise prices faster than experience curve costs to cause the smallest producers to grow fastest. Lower prices faster than experience curve costs to shakeout all except a few competitors. These relationships are not affected by inflation. However, inflation has the effect of an automatic price cut if you do not raise dollar prices.

Significant inflation cannot be offset by growth except in a few fast-growth products. Therefore, constant prices in current dollars means an automatic competitive shakeout for most products. Even maintaining margins in slow-growth products requires upward price leadership by some competitor. Failure to raise prices during inflation is, in fact, a price war of attrition.

The effects of price changes are unequal. Small-share competitors are characteristically high-cost producers. Failure to increase prices is very punishing to them. Failure to increase prices during inflation naturally tends to concentrate market share in the already leading producer.

However, if one competitor increases prices and no others follow suit, the competitor holding prices constant will tend to gain share rapidly — often fast enough to offset the lower price. If the price differential is allowed to continue for an extended period, the growth in volume will lead eventually to an improvement in relative cost for the competitor gaining share. This can actually more than offset the price decrease on trend if capacity is added fast enough to keep lead time short.

It is ironic that public policy calls for holding prices steady during inflation. The result must inevitably be the squeezing out of the higher cost and smaller competitors. The same action in the absence of inflation would be viewed as extremely aggressive.

The corporate strategist must first decide whether market share is worth buying before he can evaluate pricing strategy. Inflation does offer the leading producer a chance to lower real prices methodically and slowly squeeze out higher cost competition. This can be done by just holding prices constant.

This is no small opportunity. True prices can be steadily reduced this way. In a noninflationary environment, the same result would require a series of highly visible steps that would provoke very strong reaction from competitors and perhaps from antitrust administrators.

Experience curves and inflation work in oppostie directions. In the absence of inflation, the leading producer tends to hold prices up in the face of declining costs until his loss of market share becomes unbearable. His very size provides the opportunity to maintain a price umbrella. With inflation every producer is automatically the price leader on the down side until he takes specific action to raise prices.

Passive price behavior by the leading producer means that without inflation he keeps prices too high for his own good in fast-growth situations. He loses share steadily and prices eventually decline anyhow.

Passive price behavior by the leading producer in modest and slow-growth industries during inflation means that the price is steadily lowered below the level of competitors' costs. Competitors cannot raise prices to offset inflation unless the leading producer follows suit.

Inflation changes the direction in which active price decisions must be made. However, inflation does not change the fact that there is an equilibrium price at which market share will stay constant. Either higher or lower levels will cause share to shift. Inflation makes the equilibrium price a moving target with an upward bias.

PRICES MUST EXCEED INFLATION

Prices must go up faster than inflation. Return on assets must increase faster than inflation. Failure leads first to change in financial policies, then to elimination of the higher cost competitors, and finally to shortage.

Inflation is financial growth. It is not enough for prices to increase parallel to inflation. They must go up enough to provide financing for the increased valuation of assets, as well as cover increased costs.

A company faced with a 10-percent increase in inflation rate must increase its rate of growth in assets an added 10-percent annually. That requires an additional 10-percent net return on the assets used. This is true even if there is no change in physical volume growth.

Inflation financing can come from reduced dividends, increased debt, or increased profit margin. Suppose percentage profit margin does not increase. Debt financing becomes far more difficult with inflation. Interest rates rise with inflation and rise even more if monetary restraint is used. High interest makes larger margins of profit necessary for a given amount of debt to support itself.

Reduction in dividends without faster physical growth is merely proof of financial starvation.

The marginal company is the first to feel inflation. Its past survival against lower cost competitors depended on those competitors' self-restraint, in the form of dividend payout instead of growth, of low debt instead of lower prices.

Thus, inflation turns the low-cost competitor into a marginal competitor if profit margins are not raised. It turns the high-cost competitor into a shrinking competitor if the profit margins are held down.

Truly marginal competitors rarely pay a dividend. They have little unused debt capacity. They can grow as fast as their competitors only by paying lower dividends and issuing a larger proportion of debt. Deny them this, and they must fall behind because of financial starvation.

Higher inflation may well be with us for a long time. If you are an investor, beware of the high Beta shares which have a lower ROA than the industry leader. Invest in industry leaders even if profits are down, particularly if they are gaining market share. Subtract inflation from current return on net work (after taxes) to find the real performance index.

If you are the manager of a low margin company, get your long-term credit lined up — fast. If you are the manager of an industry leader, now is the time to choose your future. You can hold your historic percentage profit margin, use your debt capacity to maintain adequate capacity, and shake off much of your competition. If you prefer more short-term profit at the expense of future profits and market share, then raise prices now faster than inflation. This will protect your competitors, as well as cause public censure for inflationary pricing.

Of course, if you hold traditional profit margins, you will tend to become a monopolist and that will bring public censure, too. Take your choice. An increase in inflation will force you to choose.

A period of high inflation is a period in which each company must choose its future. It is a time of truth in strategy decision.

PRICE POLICY

Price increases are instant additions to profit margin. Price decreases are instant decreases in margin for everyone. That is the immediate effect. The longer term effect is quite different.

Prices which increase profit margin invite entry of new competitors, expansion of capacity, and price competition. Prices which narrow profit margin discourage investment and lead to fewer competitors.

Since all competitors do not have the same costs, the changes in margin do not have the same influence on investment decision. Low margins go with low share of market. Therefore, low share causes increased sensitivity to price level.

Since the high share competitor usually has the lowest costs, he has an option. He can either maintain share and margin, or increase margin but lose share. This is not an obvious or easy choice. It depends on such factors as industry growth rate, alternative investment opportunities, and relative market shares. It is actually a choice available *only* to the high share low-cost producer. His return is greater; his margin is greater. His range of options is greater than all others. The low share competitor cannot hold a price umbrella. He loses share too fast if he tries.

Prices should parallel costs when market shares are stable. This seems to be an observable fact which is generally true. Market shares are usually unstable under all other conditions. Characteristically, costs follow a pattern described by the experience curve. Typically, costs in constant monetary units go down between 20 and 30 percent when accumulated experience doubles.

Experience curve costs are expressed in *constant* monetary units — that is, after adjusting for inflation. Therefore, constant margins may mean either rising or falling prices in *current* monetary units. As a rule of thumb, real costs decline about 1 percent for each 3 percent of annual growth in physical volume. That is why almost all current prices must rise. Inflation offsets cost declines in all except the most rapidly growing products.

Virtually all products and services follow a characteristic set of price patterns based on these relationships. Consequently, it is possible to predict price behavior, net of inflation, by identifying the current phase of the pattern. Conversely, it is possible to predict shifts in market share by identification of the price pattern.

The managerial economic issue remains the same: which is more valuable — higher profit margin now or higher market share in the future? This is an investment decision.

THE PRICING PARADOX

The profit equation has three variables — price, volume, and cost. Of these, price is the most common candidate for manipulation since nothing else need change to produce profits for all competitors, provided they all change prices together. That togetherness is what gives birth to dreams of "industry statesmanship" as a means of achieving better profits through higher prices.

In fact, both volume and cost are easier to change than industry price levels. Efforts to change prices can cause them to ebb and flow like the tide, with equal net effect on mean sea level. Above-normal prices inevitably attract additional capacity until prices become depressed. Depressed prices inhibit capacity replacement or additions until prices rise. This is a corollary of the economic truism that competition will force prices down to approach costs, or it will cause costs to rise to approach prices.

The consequences of a price advance are predictable. At best, other producers will follow the leader and there will be a substantial price rise. But this in turn sets up a ready-made umbrella for the new capacity of these other competitors, which *must* force their way into the market to fill their added capacity.

The usual result is an artificial list price which hides real price cuts at the expense of the market leader. Because of the price leader's price rise, its profit erosion is obscured temporarily until it is decided at some later date that the company must retain its share of market. In the meantime, it has subsidized the invasion of its market share by competitors and justified their investment in more capacity.

In the short term, the others may not follow this price leadership. Consequently, the leader must not only retract the price increase, but also suffer some market volume loss.

Over the longer term, the consequences are quite different. The share of the market is determined by what company has the capacity and can use it fully. In the long term, the maintenance or addition of capacity is nearly always a function of past profits and their effect on profit expectations in the future.

Over the long term, profit and profit expectations are based upon anticipated relative costs and operating rates. As a consequence, short-term higher prices for the industry tend to encourage capacity additions and provide the cash flow to justify that expansion.

This is simply classic economics, but the strategic implications are not immediately obvious:

> *If you have the lowest cost at nominal capacity,* then it is to your advantage to keep prices down sufficiently at all times to dissuade competition from making additional capacity investments, unless, of course, you can raise prices and still stay at nominal capacity.
>
> Also, it is to your advantage to invest in added capacity as long as you can do so and maintain your cost advantage. This requires that the added capacity be operated at a load factor high enough to provide cost levels no higher than competitors' average cost. In fact, in an active technology you must make capacity additions to maintain a cost advantage.

If your fixed costs are higher but your operating costs are lower than those of competitors, then you are more sensitive to changes in operating rate. It is to your advantage to accept any kind of short-term price derpession which provides a high operating rate. Only under these conditions can you maintain a relative cost advantage. For the same reason, you can accept a lower price level without out-of-pocket loss than your competitors can. This situation is usually true of the new facility.

If your company is the low-cost producer with the newest facilities, then any price which is required to operate your facility at nominal capacity is not only justified, but is a prerequisite for maintaining your relative cost advantage. Any higher price is relatively disadvantageous. Conversely, high-cost producers must keep prices high or obtain a higher operating rate.

Competitive strategy comes into play in the effort to induce competitors to accept practices which shift *relative* costs. The corporate strategist with the new low-cost facility must persuade competitors that he can and will depress prices indefinitely — until prices are below their cost, if need be — to the point that the new facility is operating at average industry capacity. In fact, he has the power to do this. He benefits most, however, if he does not need to depress prices to fill his new capacity.

The strategist who has higher cost facilities but is in possession of the market must convince competitors that high prices for the industry are to everyone's advantage. In this way, he can offset his relative cost disadvantage. He may also find it necessary to convince competitors that it will be too costly to wrest his existing market share by price action. If he can induce competitors to use a nonprice means of competing, then their added costs may defer for a long time their realization of the inherent advantage of newer and more efficient capacity.

In the short term, the really critical elements of strategy are those which induce a competitor, for whatever reason, to accept a lower operating rate. This imposes a relative cost handicap which has no offsetting virtues.

In the long term, the critical elements are those which determine the willingness of competitors to make further capital investment in capacity. Any uncertainty, risk, or competitive policy which can delay this kind of decision produces a higher profit level on average for those already in production.

Viewed in this light:

Short-term price increases tend to depress industry profits in the long-term by accelerating the introduction of new capacity and depressing market demand.

Short-term price increases favor the high-cost producer relatively more than the low-cost producer.

The lower cost producer has everything to gain and little to lose by depressing prices until the company is operating at nominal capacity.

The perfect strategy for the low-cost producer is one which persuades others to permit him to obtain maximum use of capacity with minimum price depression — at the others' expense in terms of operating rate and profit.

The perfect strategy for the high-cost producer is one which persuades others that market shares cannot be shifted except over long periods of time, and, therefore, that the highest practical industry prices are to everyone's advantage.

Paradoxically, it is often the strongest and lowest cost producer which leads the way in establishing higher prices, even though the company itself may be operating below optimum capacity. When this happens, it must be considered a strategic victory for the higher cost producer in the market.

If all of this seems obvious, it is difficult to explain the concern of businessmen, security analysts, and others with industry price levels. It would appear that the factor of vital concern should be relative costs — or, rather, relative profit margins. The focus on short-term profits, which are often transient, frequently influences long-term performance in the opposite way from that desired.

PATTERN FOR SUCCESS

Successful companies make almost all of their profit from products in which they dominate the relevant market. Usually their market share for these products exceeds the combined share of the next two competitors. This seems to be true no matter how large or small the company, and in spite of U.S. antitrust philosophy.

But this characteristic pattern for success is not always obvious. Identical products do not necessarily serve identical markets, and different markets may have quite different distribution methods and costs. However, when products and markets are properly defined, it becomes apparent that there are only a few significant competitors in any given market for a given product.

The most profitable producers are those which dominate the market segments they serve. Conversely, when a company does not clearly dominate a product market segment, its profit margin is distinctly inferior to that of the producer that does dominate.

This pattern should surprise no one. Pareto's Law states that most of the volume should be concentrated in a few producers. Experience curve theory shows that the producer with the largest market share should have the lowest cost. It follows that the products with the largest volume and lowest costs should provide most of the profit.

If profit margin is a function of market share, then market share becomes very valuable. Investment in market share is worthwhile when the market is growing rapidly and the value of market share is being rapidly multiplied.

The most rewarding way to obtain market share is to acquire it early. This requires early recognition of the large-growth product, as well as early commitment to the investment required to obtain and hold the dominant share during the growth period. The return on such an investment can be very high indeed when the product becomes mature. The earlier the investment is made, the higher the return for leadership will be. This is why R&D can pay off so handsomely, even with the uncertainty and long delay before there is a return.

Company success requires a series of products. Products must eventually mature. When they do, they provide the cash flow for investment in a new series of high-potential, high growth products. Thus, mature products fund investment in market share of growth products until they, too, become mature and the cycle can be repeated.

This seems to be the pattern successful companies follow. The implications are far-reaching. Those who understand the underlying logic, and can control their investments accordingly, have the opportunity to achieve and sustain high levels of growth and profitability. Those who do not understand the full consequences of this pattern will constantly exchange long-term success for short-term improvements in current performance.

CAPACITY

The timing of capacity additions determines both market share and profitability. Lack of capacity at peak demand inevitably means loss of market share to those companies which do have capacity. Excess capacity means added cost with no benefit.

Capacity must be added before it is needed. Adding capacity requires time: to plan, to build, and to debug. For this reason, capacity additions must always be started well before capacity is needed.

Capacity is the determinant of market share. Inadequate capacity means long lead times at best, and perhaps sales lost forever. Differences in lead time are a compelling motive for changing suppliers. The resulting change in market share is often permanent. The size of the backlog is a measure of the probable loss in market share.

---

* The public interest *requires* the concentration of production and distribution in the minimum practical number of competitors. This is necessary to achieve the lowest consumer prices and the highest national productivity.

Characteristically, if the size of the smallest effective competitor's market share is doubled, the price to the user should be expected to approach a level about 25 percent lower than it could have been otherwise. This can occur without affecting the profit margin of that producer.

The public is served best by concentration of marketing and distribution in a few producers for any given product, whether the companies involved are large or small. Unfortunately, it requires a diversified company to provide the capital necessary to develop and market a rapidly growing product at the rate which is optimum for both the company and the product users. Consequently, the most desirable situation from the users' point of view would be vigorous competition among a few large-scale, diversified companies that rapidly dominate the markets for their products.

Shift of market share is the basis for a shift in relative cost. Therefore, a loss of market share can be and often is a permanent loss of future profit margin, even though output continues to grow and existing capacity is normally utilized.

A competitor in a growth business will automatically lose market share if capacity additions are delayed until existing capacity is fully required. Any industry growth while your own company's capacity is fixed and fully used is by definition a proportionate loss of your share.

However, market share is always lost to a competitor. His capacity had to be in existence for you to lose share to him. Therefore, his decisions on timing of capacity additions determine his delivery capability versus your own. Delivery capability is far more often a determinant of market share shift than price competition itself.

The surest way to gain market share, other things being relatively normal, is to persuade your competitor *not* to invest in added capacity at the same time that you do so. But since your ability to inhibit competitive investment must be indirect by nature, then the real battle is in the mind of your competitor. Your initiative in adding capacity affects your competitor's subsequent decision. Capacity, once created, is irreversible in cost commitment.

The competitor who adds capacity first may not make a profit, but the competitor who lags the leader cannot win, whether or not he eventually adds capacity. Price competition is thus a psychological weapon that affects investment choices, not a means of attacking or taking business away from competitors.

Know your competitor's investment decision rules and patterns. Manage your competitor's investment decisions by your own initiative in adding capacity before it is needed.

THE MARKET SHARE PARADOX

Market share is very valuable. It leads to lower relative cost and, therefore, higher profits. Unfortunately, most efforts to improve market share depress profits, at least in the short term.

There are two principal reasons for a shift in market share between competitors. The more common is lack of capacity. The other reason is a willingness to lose share to maintain price.

Lack of capacity is a common problem, because it is expensive
to maintain unused capacity for very long. Even in the face of projected *industry* growth, it is not surprising that not all *individual*
producers feel they can justify the incremental investment in added
capacity. On the other hand, nothing is more obvious than the fact
that capacity limits market share. If the market grows and capacity
does not, then the company which has the capacity takes the growth,
and increases its share of the market — at your expense.

The decision to add capacity is a fateful one. Add too soon,
and extra costs are incurred with no benefits. Add too late, and
market share is lost. Added capacity means more than bricks and
machines. It also means capable personnel in the proper proportions in the proper places. Because the lead time required is long,
the decision must anticipate the need.

The competitive implications are made more complex by the
cost differentials among competitors. Simple arithmetic shows that
the high-cost producer must add capacity in direct proportion to
the low-cost firm, if relative market shares are to remain constant.
But the high-cost producer's return on the capacity investment is
lower than that of the more efficient firm, because of the difference
in profit margins.

The market share paradox is that if the low-cost firm would
accept the high-cost producer's return on assets, the low-cost firm
would pre-empt all market growth. The resulting increase in the
latter's accumulated experience would further improve its costs and
thereafter steadily increase the cost *differential* between the competitors.

**In short, if the same investment criteria were used by all firms,
then the low-cost firm would always expand capacity first
and other firms never would.**

However, all firms do *not* use the same investment criteria.
The fact that market share is stable proves this. However, this also
means that shares are unstable if there is vigorous competition.

The low-cost producer can only take market share if he is
willing to sacrifice near-term profit. The high-cost producer can
obtain a significant return only because he is allowed to do so in
order to maintain current prices.

The tradeoff is inviting. Since the low-cost firm typically has
the largest market share, higher expectations for return often lead it

to sacrifice share to maintain near-term margins. The loss of a modest amount of the market may seem far less costly in the short-term than meeting a price concession of a minor competitor, or spreading the price reduction necessary to fill proposed new capacity over the firm's entire sales volume.

Unfortunately, the tradeoff is cumulative. More and more share must be given up over time to maintain price. Costs are a function of market share because of the experience effect. Lost market share leads to loss of cost advantage. Eventually, there is no way to maintain profitability.

The rate of growth is the critical variable in resolving the market share paradox and the tradeoff between share and near-term profits.

> Without growth, it is virtually impossible to shift market share. Competitors can neither justify adding capacity, nor afford to lose share at the price of idle capacity. Under such constraints, since prices will tend to be very stable, the appropriate strategy is to maximize profits within existing market shares.

> With little growth, a higher near-term profit may be worth considerably more than continued modest profit. The only competitors which should hold share into the no-growth period are those with enough share — and the resulting cost position — to anticipate satisfactory profits.

> With rapid growth, market share is both very valuable and very easy to lose. On the one hand, any improvement in share will be compounded by growth of the market itself, and then again by improved margins as cost improvement accrues from increased volume and, hence, experience. On the other hand, growth means that capacity must be added rapidly, in advance of the growth, or share will be lost automatically; to gain share, capacity addition must be based on pre-empting the growth component.

Any shift in market share should be regarded as either investment or disinvestment. The rate of return can and should be evaluated just as it would be in any other business situation.

Change in market share should be an investment decision.

INDUSTRIAL PRICING POLICY AND
MARKET SHARE

Price policy is usually established at the highest management levels in a company. Yet there are few management decisions that are more subject to intuition and more clearly
the product of corporate mythology.

There is a reason for this. All price decisions are based on
assumptions about what a competitor will do under certain
hypothetical circumstances. There is no way to know that for
sure — hence, the characteristic reliance on intuition.

Yet there *is* a logic to competitive behavior. In addition,
there is abundant evidence that industrial prices follow certain
kinds of patterns that are stable over long periods of time,
regardless of what competitors try to do. If there is a logic and
a rationale for this pattern, then there is a basis for analysis
and predictions of the consequences of changing a given price.
What follows is an example of that kind of analysis.

We start with the assumption that prices are set on the basis
of constraints determined by competition. Assume also that each
competitor will be unable or unwilling to sell below cost for any
protracted period of time. This leads to the obvious conclusion that
most of the competitors in any given product market area will be
operating at a high percentage of their capacity. In other words,
only a modest proportion of their organization and facilities are not
being put to use. In a growing economy this means that each producer must periodically add to its capacity or it will lose market
share.

This decision to add to capacity is a fateful one. Additional
funds are being committed to the business. The risk and exposure
are compounded. But competitive position will be affected adversely if the capacity is not added.

If we assume that all producers do not have the same costs,
why is it that the most profitable producer does not add capacity
first and pre-empt all of the growth? The question can be stated
another way: what is it that keeps investment decisions in step with
each other and, therefore, keeps market shares constant? We do
assume that all producers have the same equivalent price level,
whether or not they have the same cost levels.

If prices are the same but costs are different, each producer must have a different return on new capacity investment. But why will one demand more return before investing than others? Is there some reason to assume that each producer cannot change its share of the market if it adds capacity first?

The answer is that there is no reason why not, if the producer then has capacity and its competitors do not. The answer is the opposite, however, if all competitors have adequate capacity at all times. How, indeed, would share change if all suppliers were equal?

Consider the hypothesis that market share almost never changes hands between two competent competitors unless one has inadequate capacity while the other does not.

It is a generally accepted fact that competitors will meet price competition at once and meet nonprice competition as soon as they realize that they are being hurt. If this is true, then there is no way for market share to change except by mistake or because of lack of capacity. This leads to the conclusion that the real role of price level is to determine which product is willing to add capacity first, and when its competitors will be willing to follow.

This view of the competitive world casts the low-cost producer in the role of the giant with the whip hand. It casts the high-cost producer in the role of the challenger whose decisions to invest and take risks in the face of the giant's cost advantage will determine the price level. Two different scenarios in the competitive drama are possible.

In the first scenario, the giant with the lower cost is faced with large reductions in price and, therefore, in profit, in order to prevent the smaller and higher cost producer from adding capacity. The smaller producer does in fact add the capacity. However, to do so requires a price differential, or its equivalent in added cost for added services, to attract the added volume. The larger and more efficient competitor permits the price differential or equivalent to exist rather than take the substantial loss in near-term profit that would be necessary to prevent the shift. However, the added capacity and growth of the high-cost producer leads to an improvement in the relative cost positions. Thus, the entire process is repeated until the former small, high-cost producer becomes the dominant, large, low-cost producer. In this scenario there is no shortage of capacity, but the low-cost producer prefers immediate payout to future market share and profitability.

The second scenario unfolds if the low-cost producer adds capacity as necessary in order to maintain market share and then does whatever is necessary to fill this capacity and maintain market share. If this is strictly adhered to, the high-cost producer still sets the actual level of prices. There is no way that the high-cost producer can buy market share because the low-cost producer will not let that happen. If the high-cost producer does not add any capacity, there will be a shortage as the industry grows. The leader has only provided added capacity in proportion to its own share. The shortage raises prices. When the return becomes attractive enough, then the high-cost producer does indeed add more capacity and relieve the shortage, thus setting the price level.

This series of events is highly stable. The profit margin required for the high-cost producer to be induced to invest determines the price level for the industry and the rate of return for all competitors. The actual profit margin of the high-cost producer usually turns out to be just enough to finance the growth in capacity required to hold position, but not enough to permit any significant amount of capital to be taken out as dividends to the owners of the business.

There is a third possible scenario. Suppose that the high- and low-cost producers are willing to accept the same return on investment. The relationship between competitors becomes increasingly unstable. As the market grows, the low-cost producer will pre-empt all the growth because it will be the only competitor that adds capacity as the need grows. However, its costs will go down with its rapidly accumulating market share and experience. A peculiar thing happens. Over time both the market share and the profit margin of the low-cost producer widen, even though prices are still so low that the other producers cannot justify adding any capacity.

Several factors make this last scenario, as a strategy, rather unusual in practice:

Accounting conventions tend to overstate the costs compared to the trend line average during the early phases of a new capacity addition. This inhibits investment until the need and the opportunity become obvious to all, including the higher cost producers.

Business conventions have established return on assets as the goal, instead of return on equity or growth in the business. This tends to bias investment decisions toward maintenance of the status quo, rather than aggressive pursuit of position in the future.

Management accountability of the publicly held, professionally managed company puts rather heavy emphasis on reported earnings in the present, rather than on the present value of future earnings that may be the actual result. The "bird-in-the-hand-is-worth-two-in-the-bush" concept naturally tends to dominate.

The interesting aspect, however, is that under certain circumstances the willingness to add capacity and depress prices can lead to very handsome returns on investment, particularly in fast-growing product areas. Whether this occurs depends upon the investment policies of competitors, not upon their price policies.

Price policies, it appears, are in fact a product of investment policies. Conversely, it appears that true consequence of price changes is to affect the investment decisions of competitors.

Price changes do affect short-term profitability of all competitors equally as a percentage of sales. But in the long run, it appears that only the investment return standards determine prices or profits. The strategist who is willing to invest when others are not sets the price level for everyone by virtue of that investment.

NEW PRODUCT PRICING

The prospects of an exciting new product are often destroyed by a conventional introductory pricing strategy. Early market domination is much more valuable than most companies realize, and internal compromises on initial pricing tactics are frequently disastrous to long-term profitability.

The basic objective in pricing a new product should be to prevent competitors from gaining experience and market share before the new product has achieved major volume. If this is done, it is possible to achieve a cost advantage over competitors which cannot ever profitably be overcome by normal performance on the part of competitors.

Unit costs are necessarily very high in the early stages of any product. In many cases, a product may not find a market if it has to be sold at its initial cost in competition with existing alternative products. However, if prices are set at a level which will move the product, then costs come down with experience. This means, of course, that operations are conducted at a loss until costs decline below that initial price.

Ignoring competition, there is an optimum initial price which may well be below initial cost. It must be low enough to find a market. If the market is at all price sensitive, there are some major advantages to forcing the development of the market as rapidly as is practical, and thus compressing the time required to get volume up and costs down. Assume, however, that the market growth rate is unaffected by the price policy of individual competitors. Market elasticity simply exaggerates the results of pricing actions, since lowering prices usually increases the total market, as well as participation in market growth.

In the absence of competition, there would be every reason to set prices as high as possible and lower them only when volume times margin would be increased by lowering price. This approach is often adopted, even though it can be a serious mistake if potentially strong competition exists. Indeed, in a competitive market, and assuming that a new product has substantial potential for future volume, the competitive cost differential in the future should be of greater concern than current profitability.

The lower the initial price set by the first producer, the more rapidly that company builds up volume and a differential cost advantage over succeeding competitors, and the faster the market develops. In a sense, this is a purchase of time advantage. However, the lower the initial price, the greater the investment required before the progressive reduction of cost will result in a profit. This means that, once again, the comparative investment resources of the competitors involved can become a significant, or even the critical, determinant of competitive survival.

It is even conceivable that the financial resources required to follow this type of initial pricing strategy may exceed those available to the firm. This apparently happened with the supersonic transport. Even when one firm can supply the financial resources required, the sum required may be so large that failure in the strategy would bankrupt the firm.

In addition to financial resources, another limit on extremely low initial prices is that set by the potential return on investment. Assuming that the price, once set, will not be raised but will be maintained until costs fall below it, the lower the price, the longer the time that any return is deferred and the larger the investment. When future cost differentials are discounted to present value, there is an obvious limit.

However, under ordinary circumstances the future growth of the market is uncertain. Consequently, initial prices tend to be set on initial costs in the absence of clear competitive threats. As volume builds up and costs decline, this normally produces visible profitability, which, in turn, induces new competitors to enter the field. The market leader now has the classic problem of choosing between current profitability and market share.

It should also be pointed out that, characteristically, it is impractical to attempt to take physical volume away from a competitor. The critical stake is ordinarily the share of the growth of the market. Once the product matures enough so that its annual growth in volume ceases, then all of the preceding discussion is essentially academic.

Pricing of a new product is of critical importance because it determines the participation possible in that product's future growth. For the product with a real future, this is obviously far more important than near-term profitability.

Most businessmen are intuitively aware of the tradeoffs which must be made when a new product is introduced. Miscalculations result from the uncertainties involved and the difficulty of justifying short-term losses in return for future market position. Fortunately, with the discovery of cost-experience relationships, it is now possible to deal quantitatively with the principal tradeoffs. Cost is related in constant terms to cumulative volume and that, in turn, is related to market share. Understanding these relationships has enabled businessmen to focus on the major issues in new product introduction and to set appropriate price levels with greater confidence than in the past.

THE PRODUCT PORTFOLIO

To be successful, a company should have a portfolio of products with different growth rates and different market shares. The portfolio composition is a function of the balance between cash flows. High-growth products require cash inputs to grow. Low-growth products should generate excess cash. Both kinds are needed simultaneously.

Four rules determine the cash flow of a product:

> Margins and cash generated are a function of market share. High margins and high market share go together. This is a matter of common observation, explained by the experience curve effect.
>
> Growth requires cash input to finance added assets. The added cash required to hold share is a function of growth rates.
>
> High market share must be earned or bought. Buying market share requires additional investment.
>
> No product market can grow indefinitely. The payoff from growth must come when the growth slows, or it will not come at all. The payoff is cash that cannot be reinvested in that product.

Products with high market share and slow growth are "cash cows." Characteristically, they generate large amounts of cash, in excess of the reinvestment required to maintain share. This excess need not, and should not, be reinvested in those products. In fact, if the rate of return exceeds the growth rate, the cash *cannot* be reinvested indefinitely, except by depressing returns.

Products with low market share and slow growth are "dogs." They may show an accounting profit, but the profit must be reinvested to maintain share, leaving no cash throwoff. The product is essentially worthless, except in liquidation.

All products eventually become either a "cash cow" or a "dog." The value of a product is completely dependent upon obtaining a leading share of its market before the growth slows.

Low market share, high-growth products are the "problem children." They almost always require far more cash than they can generate. If cash is not supplied, they fall behind and die. Even when the cash is supplied, if they only hold their share, they are still dogs when the growth stops. The "problem children" require large added cash investment for market share to be purchased. The low market share, high-growth product is a liability unless it becomes a leader. It requires very large cash inputs that it cannot generate itself.

THE MATRIX
Market Share

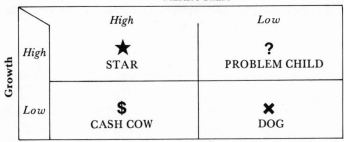

OPTIMUM CASH FLOW
Market Share

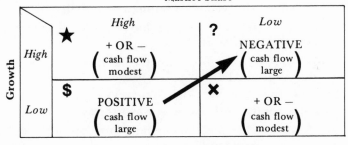

SUCCESS SEQUENCE
Market Share

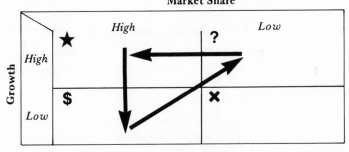

DISASTER SEQUENCE
Market Share

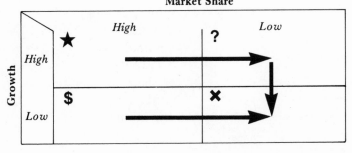

The high share, high growth product is the "star." It nearly always shows reported profits, but it may or may not generate all of its own cash. If it stays a leader, however, it will become a large cash generator when growth slows and its reinvestment requirements diminish. The star eventually becomes the cash cow — providing high volume, high margin, high stability, security — and cash throwoff for reinvestment elsewhere.

The payoff for leadership is very high indeed, if it is achieved early and maintained until growth slows. Investment in market share during the growth phase can be very attractive — if you have the cash. Growth in market is compounded by growth in share. Increases in share increase the margin. Higher margin permits higher leverage with equal safety. The resulting profitability permits higher payment of earnings after financing normal growth. The return on investment is enormous.

The need for a portfolio of businesses becomes obvious. Every company needs products in which to invest cash. Every company needs products that generate cash. And every product should eventually be a cash generator; otherwise, it is worthless.

Only a diversified company with a balanced portfolio can use its strengths to truly capitalize on its growth opportunities. The balanced portfolio has:

"stars," whose high share and high growth assure the future;

"cash cows," that supply funds for that future growth; and

"problem children," to be converted into "stars" with the added funds.

"Dogs" are not necessary. They are evidence of failure either to obtain a leadership position during the growth phase, or to get out and cut the losses.

VI

OTHER FORCES AND
CORPORATE MANAGEMENT

6

ANTITRUST POLICY

Most Americans favor competition — they are opposed to monopoly and they fear government regulation. They see no acceptable alternative to current antitrust policy, since direct government regulation of business by administrative decree seems to be the other alternative. That implies the red tape, frustration, delay, and inflexibility of bureaucracy everywhere.

Yet there is a disquieting amount of evidence that the underlying assumptions of antitrust policy should be re-examined and re-appraised. Perhaps the consumer is being forced to pay much more than he should. Perhaps the cost of production is higher than it needs to be. The national standard of living and productivity may be unnecessarily penalized.

America is famous for mass production and the resulting low costs. This is not surprising in view of the fact that the U.S. has by far the world's largest unimpeded, unencumbered and accessible market. The question, however, is: what costs are incurred by forcing production to be divided among two, four, eight, or sixteen independent producers, instead of letting competition gradually eliminate the less efficient until there is a high concentration?

Experience curve theory says that a single producer should eventually achieve costs for a given product that are about 75 percent of the potential cost of two otherwise equivalent and equally competent producers who share the same market:

about (0.75×0.75) — 56% of four equal but independent equivalents, or
$(0.75 \times 0.75 \times 0.75)$ — 42% of the cost of eight, or
$(0.75 \times 0.75 \times 0.75 \times 0.75)$ — 31% of sixteen producers

The experience curve hypothesis is theoretical and there may be some major exceptions. The implications are still far reaching.

The implication of antitrust policy is that prices must be kept high enough to protect the smallest and least experienced producer, otherwise there would eventually be a monopoly as, one by one, the less efficient were displaced. Yet it might be better to let Western Electric make a large profit margin, rather than raising prices enough to support four competing telephone manufacturers. There is some circumstantial evidence that aluminum costs might be half what they are if Alcoa still had a U.S. monopoly. (See chart which follows.)

What is it worth to avoid direct government intervention in the price level? Is it worth doubling (or more) the cost of production and distribution?

Antitrust policy appears to be vacillating between two mutually exclusive philosophies. One is to protect competitors, particularly small ones, the other is to protect competition. Protecting competitors means protecting them against competition. You cannot protect competition and competitors simultaneously.

Effective competition means that market shares are by definition unstable until some competitor is clearly dominant. Failure to concentrate production in a dominant producer is per se evidence of ineffective competition.

There is a large amount of evidence, again circumstantial, that eventually all products tend to settle into a market share pattern in which there is a very high correlation between market share and profit margin. The only exceptions appear to be where there is collusion, government restraint of competition or control of natural resources. Even the smallest company makes most of its profit in the specific products in which it is the dominant, or at least a leading producer. Any other pattern is highly unstable. Product by product, this seems to be true now in spite of antitrust.

If there is a direct correlation between market share and cost, then it can be very costly to the consumer to keep prices high enough to protect and preserve more than a few producers of any given product.

Business is not an end in itself. It is merely the mechanism for efficiently carrying out the national objectives. The laws and government policies which deal with business should be designed so that business can realize the national objectives while pursuing its own interests. The starting point is the national objectives, one of which is to increase the national productivity and standard of living.

Almost everyone will agree that it is desirable for business to produce and deliver at the lowest achievable cost. It is equally obvious that capital investment should be made in the areas where it is the most productive. Low costs should be passed on to the consumer in low prices — or used to generate capital which is reinvested — or converted into taxable income which permits the government to siphon off half of it and direct the employment of the benefits. All three do happen. But each beneficiary is dependent upon the development of low costs.

Antitrust policy is based on a widely held American conviction that competition spurs maximum effort and eliminates the inefficient producer. Certainly competition tends to do these things. But the efficient producer must make a big profit or the less efficient producer cannot make any. Consequently, the consumer must pay prices equal to the cost of the least efficient producer. Also, if the most efficient producer passes low costs on to the customer, he will eventually eliminate all of his competition. The consumer must pay high prices unless production is concentrated in the most efficient producer.

These relationships would exist even if size or scale were no factor in costs. Yet, scale clearly is a factor in most businesses; the consumer is severely penalized by protection or preservation of the small-scale producer from larger and more effective competitors.

If a large, efficient competitor charges a high price and makes a large profit, then at least it generates a lot of capital, about half of which the government will appropriate by taxation. If that same production were spread among a number of smaller and less profitable competitors, the economy would suffer, even though the sales price remained the same.

Antitrust policy should, above all, be directed towards achieving the lowest possible cost of production and distribution. Secondarily, it could be intended to influence whether the benefits of low cost are passed on to the consumer, the employees, the equity shareholders, or the government. It is not clear what is best in this respect. However, there are many ways for government to redirect the benefits of low-cost production without interfering significantly with the ability to achieve low costs.

Current antitrust policy is of questionable value in developing a more efficient economy. It appears that consumers are paying more than they need to, the economy is generating less reinvestable capital and the government is collecting less taxes because of an antitrust policy which protects inefficient producers from competition. Much of America's natural advantage in having the largest unimpeded market can be dissipated by protecting inefficient units from efficient ones.

What is antitrust for?

**THE PEIRATIC CURVE* FOR PRIMARY ALUMINUM
1929 - 1966**

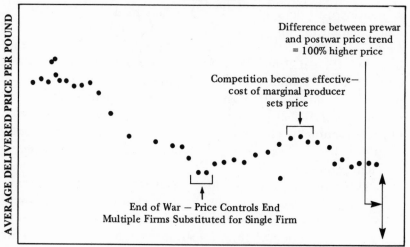

**INDUSTRY TOTAL ACCUMULATED VOLUME
(thousand short tons)**

*Peira, (Gk.,) Accumulated Experience

WHAT MAKES JAPAN GROW?

The Context

It is a common assumption that the growth of the Japanese economy is based primarily upon low labor costs. Nothing could be further from the truth. Many parts of Asia have far lower labor costs, as well as far more raw material.

The secret of Japanese growth lies in three factors:

1. the methods of financing growth
2. the Japanese culture and educational system
3. the government-business relationship

None of these is temporary. The foundations of Japanese industrial growth are sound. Japanese industrial productivity can easily become the greatest in the world in the next generation unless more favored nations learn lessons from Japan.

Japanese business practices and culture are far different from those of any Western nation. This has obscured recognition of the nearly ideal conditions that Japan has created for corporate growth. These conditions affect both the firm itself and its relationship to other firms, to its markets, and to the government.

The first requirement for growth is capital. In the case of Japanese companies, a large part of the capital is supplied by bank loans — a practice that would be extremely dangerous and unthinkable in most countries. It is neither in Japan; instead, it is a source of great strength.

Characteristically, most Japanese companies have debt ratios of 80 percent or even more. This means that, for practical purposes, they do not have to finance their growth out of retained earnings. If they earn enough to cover the interest on their debt, then there is little financial constraint on growth. This permits very small profit margins on sales to create substantial growth rates in stockholder equity.

These bank loans are essentially permanent capital, even though they are short-term obligations. The Bank of Japan stands behind the commercial bank. No major company's loan is ever likely to be called unless the Bank of Japan wants it called.

This power of the purse gives the Japanese government great power over Japanese business. This is true in many other ways as well, and can be a major growth stimulus. The Japanese government is in partnership with Japanese business. It is neither an alternative to private business, nor primarily a policeman. Rather, business is an extension of public policy by private means.

These relationships have profound influences on competition and the resulting prices. Since companies do not have to finance their growth from retained earnings, the more successful firm can grow extremely rapidly without raising prices to finance that growth.

The pressure on the marginal firm is great. The efficient firm drives out the inefficient very quickly. The banks and the government deliver the *coup de grace* by calling the loans of the less efficient firm. The net effect is a rapid concentration of production in the hands of the lowest cost producer, with the consequent benefits of scale effect and cost-volume relationships, which further lower the costs of the most efficient producer.

This concentration of production has far more profound consequences than appear on the surface. There is an overwhelming body of evidence that changes in cost are a direct function of changes in accumulated experience. For example, over time the unit cost of production of two equal producers would be 100/75, or 133 percent of that of a single concentrated producer of an item. The same production spread equally among four producers would result in a unit cost of 100/75 x 75, or 177 percent of a single producer; among eight producers it would be 100/75 x 75 x 75, or 237 percent of a single producer. Thus, the combination of rapid growth and lower cost with narrow profit margins can obviously produce highly competitive price potentials.

Labor practices in Japan are often considered by Western businessmen to be unworkable and highly restrictive. They may in fact by the opposite. The employee of the Japanese firm is employed for life, or as long as the company survives. The employee's salary is not set by the job but by age, family situation, education, and length of service. In effect, the Japanese employee is a member of a family for life, with all the mutual obligations, covenants, and privileges that this implies.

These labor practices have three major effects. First, labor cost, once incurred, is a fixed cost. Second, labor has an internal flexibility and mobility that is inconceivable to the Western manager. Third, the employee identifies with the firm in the same way he does with his own family.

If labor is viewed as a fixed cost, then the only remaining variable of consequence is raw material cost. This places extreme pressure on a Japanese firm to operate at nominal capacity as long as revenues at least cover raw material cost. This can produce export prices which are extremely low but still attractive to the Japanese producer. The domestic market is protected from external competition in such a way that it may be little affected.

The internal flexibility of the Japanese organization is far greater than its Western counterpart. Since status is not dependent on job assignment, this permits great flexibility in assignment of personnel. The rigidities of union featherbedding and work rules are almost unknown in a Japanese company.

Such flexibility and interchangeability of function are possible only if a large proportion of the labor force is literate and has a high level of general education. The labor force in Japan does have this base; the general population is among the best educated in the world.

All of these factors are favorable only in a stable economy and in a competitive climate in which the government takes a constructive role. The Japanese government's behavior goes far beyond the U.S. regulatory role or the typical European planning, yet it has little resemblance to the centralized management of socialist economies. The government is a major and direct factor in Japanese growth.

Government planning in Japan does not take the form of a detailed five-year plan, nor a French national plan. Neither is it characterized by a laissez-faire approach with restrictions, as in the U.S. Rather, the Japanese government has an economic strategy — a good one.

The Strategy

If Japan were a single corporation instead of a nation, it could be used as the best example of a well-conceived corporate strategy. However, Japanese government policies are not announced; therefore we cannot determine them except by inference. Nevertheless, indirect controls and the way they are exercised reflect the underlying strategy. It appears that the Japanese government attempts to exercise the following essential business-stabilizing functions:

Provide a flow of capital to industry through the banks which will be adequate to permit maximum overall growth in the economy but inadequate to permit "overheating," which would result in inflation and shortages.

Stabilize the rate of technological displacement of labor at a level which will permit the high-productivity/large-capital industries to absorb the displacement. This is done both by regulating capital flow and by price pressure (up or down).

Concentrate investment in those industries in which Japanese worldwide competitive capability is the greatest. This can be observed by the progression from high-labor content products, to high-precision and high-labor products, to high-technology products, to capital-intensive products. The high-growth areas of Japanese industrial expansion have been those where Japan could reasonably look forward to a strong position in worldwide trade.

Protect domestic industry from foreign competition until it is fully developed technically and in scale to be self-sufficient. This is the same objective the American colonists set up for themselves. It is quite legitimate. This is not protection of jobs since those employees displaced by imports are easily absorbed into growth sectors. More precisely, *new* employment is diverted to growth sectors.

It is not clear yet whether the Japanese government fully recognizes the need for equal trade in order to achieve full productivity. So far, exports have been essential just to obtain raw materials. Yet Japan's major trade potential must be with other developed countries. Eventually, their industrial development will require reciprocal trade of highly sophisticated manufactured goods in accordance with the law of comparative advantage. When that happens, Japan and its trading partners will become mutually dependent.

The Japanese government has come under severe criticism from both foreign governments and foreign businessmen for the maze of obstacles put in the way of the foreign investor, as well as the importer to Japan. Obviously, this is characteristic nationalism to some extent. Not so obvious, but more important, is the fact that it may be essential to the Japanese growth, at least for the present.

Japan, as an economy, is walking a tightrope:

It has a democratic form of government. This means that it is subject to popular emotions and pressure for short-term results.

It must be a trading nation because it has virtually no raw materials. Therefore, it must maintain price levels and foreign exchange flows consistent with trade while it is doubling its raw material requirement about every seven to ten years.

It must maintain internal price levels which keep internal consumption low enough to permit the massive capital formation required by the high growth rate.

All of this must be done in an external environment which is politically very complex. The major potential market is Red China. The major potential raw material supplier is Russian Siberia. The major potential customer is the U.S. All of these countries are vitally important, all are in conflict with each other, and all use their foreign business activities as an arm of foreign policy.

It is not surprising that the Japanese government, with full business support, feels that it must keep under control all the interlocking factors which affect its economy. It is not likely that this attitude will change in the forseeable future. It seems obvious that Japan will give the fewest possible hostages to a foreign government. It is also obvious that the Japanese government wants no uncontrollable foreigner to be in a position to upset this intricate balancing act.

The Future

Japan's productivity will continue to grow at its recent rate for at least another generation. It requires no great amount of faith or foresight to predict this. Although there are certain major hazards which could curtail the growth, they do not appear likely to occur. However, they are visible and appraisable.

An internal shift in government could produce a national administration with different aims and policies. This is probably unlikely in the presence of great prosperity and no external threat.

External political factors could sharply curtail the essential supply of raw material. For example, the Arab-Israeli conflict threatened Japan's oil supply.

A major diversion of effort to military applications could seriously affect the growth and stability of the industrial economy.

An upheaval in world trade or the world monetary system could disturb Japan's internal economy, which is dependent upon foreign markets.

There may be other factors which could break Japanese growth, but these are the major ones with potentially sudden or sweeping effects. Internal factors are not nearly so likely to become unfavorable.

Japan's postwar growth is similar to, but not the same as, that of Germany, Italy, and France. The assumption seems to be that Japan's growth will soon peak, as did the growth of these European industrialized countries.

Annual Increase in GNP in Real Terms[1]

	Average 1950-60	Average 1961-65	Average 1966-67
United States	3.2	4.7	4.1
Germany	7.6	4.8	1.0
Italy	5.9	5.5	5.0
France	4.7	5.1	4.0
Western Europe	4.8	4.8	2.8

Without attempting to analyze the differences in depth, it is possible to see why Japan is better able than Europe to maintain its growth rate.

Japan has relatively large reserves of labor working at low-productivity jobs which can be diverted into high-productivity jobs. The educational system facilitates this; the European system does not. Also, capital investment per laborer is still very low.

The Japanese industrial culture makes it possible to have relatively full employment without the inflation and work stoppages that invariably accompany full employment in Western nations.

The Japanese have established a differential between consumption and production which is the basic condition required for massive capital formation. Rapid growth in production permits the standard of living to increase at the same rate as production — steadily. This is not the case when an *increase* in production is attempted in an economy which is already fully using its production facilities and capital.

Incidentally, all of these things could be said about the U.S.S.R. as well. However, unlike the Japanese, the Russians have not mastered the essential skill of using the market as the sensitive control system and catalyst to establish an integrated, smoothly developing economy. The Japanese have.

The Implications

Although the above may sound like a deification of Japanese culture and economic planning, it is intended to be an objective appraisal of the probable future behavior of Japanese business. You can appraise its validity for yourself by analyzing the Japanese economy, or any other, with respect to the fundamentals required for growth in productivity.

These essentials can be summarized as follows:

The rate of new capital formation must be great enough to support the growth rate. This means that all private and public consumption, plus export, must be less than production by an amount equal to capital formation.

The capital and labor resources available must be constantly utilized to their maximum practical capacity.

The least efficient enterprises must be eliminated in favor of those which use their labor and capital most efficiently.

Artificial barriers, either political or cultural, to flexibility in the best use of human resources must be minimal. This applies particularly to work rules affecting job *assignment* and methods.

Major production activities should be concentrated in fields where the law of comparative advantage can be utilized to produce compounded consequences in cost improvement. This means the maximum use of foreign trade.

The educational system must provice a labor force adaptable to the constant change in duties and skills which characterizes rapid growth.

Workers and management must be dedicated to the health and growth of their particular company; government must show a similar dedication to overall business growth.

The Japanese culture, business practices, and government attitudes are highly favorable to business growth. This is in sharp contrast with many other industrial nations. In the U.S. there is still a high degree of hostility between government and business. Tax laws and interpretations of antitrust law are geared to prevent injury to the inefficient producer. The banking system provides no relief from the need to obtain most of the capital for growth from retained earnings. Furthermore, the political system and cultural attitudes make full employment unlikely without serious inflation. The traditional political strength of labor has been used to establish many artificial restrictions on productivity. Also, the seniority system of job *assignment* interferes with the flexibility and full use of human resources.

In Great Britain many of the U.S. problems are exaggerated as a result of the attitudes that developed when Britain was pioneering the industrial revolution. Labor practices are almost paralyzing in terms of adaptability. The educational system has a narrow base. Laws and regulations affecting business are not only cumbersome but are primarily aimed at social attitudes, without regard to their effect on national productivity.

In Italy there is essentially no capital market. The tax laws are unenforceable, but their avoidance also undermines government-business cooperation, as well as making internal control of businesses difficult.

France and Germany have well-established traditions of restricting production and capacity under cartel arrangements aimed at maintaining profit margins rather than growth or productivity.

In fact, none of the major European countries has a broad-based educational system, a stable and ready source of industrial capital, or a tradition of growth and innovation.

Certainly, Japanese industry is under no handicap compared to the other major industrialized countries. Yet the Japanese economy does have certain weaknesses which go with its strengths:

> The government is slow and reluctant to let inefficient enterprise be displaced. This is not unique to Japan; the political strength of farmers and labor has produced the same results in most countries.
>
> The lifetime tenure of employment in Japanese industry means that labor has no mobility between companies. The company which is growing faster than average must either entrust more to younger employees or curtail its growth. This may make it bolder as it grows faster.

The interlocking decision making and requirement for consensus before action can be taken could strangle Japanese business in red tape and bureaucratic politicking. So far, not only has this not been the case, it has been a source of coordination and efficient communication.

The lifetime tenure of employment also encourages very large, multiproduct companies. This, however, is at least as much a strength as it is a weakness. Within such companies, there can be considerable flexibility and internal adaptability to meet changing external conditions and opportunities.

Conclusion

For foreign businessmen, the following observations seem relevant:

Japanese growth in industrial productivity will continue. It would be surprising if it slowed up within our business generation.

The Japanese business community will continue to be a closed system, as far as foreign business is concerned.

Japanese business policies will be guided by the political posture and objectives of the Japanese government. This probably means increasing business arrangements with Red China and the U.S.S.R. These will be minimized because of their political leverage if sufficiently broad alternatives are available. However, any concentration or restriction of trade with the U.S. or Europe will increase Asiatic trade. In any case, it must be accepted as a likely parallel.

Japanese exports will be primarily a function of internal Japanese requirements in the short term. That is, facilities will be operated at or near capacity in most cases. Domestic consumption (usually at higher prices) will be satisfied first. The rest will be pushed into the export market.

Japanese business will steadily coalesce into fewer large business entities. This is the natural outcome of encouraging competition. It is also the consequence of life-tenure employment.

A greater portion of Japan's total production will be involved in foreign trade. Eventually, Japan will probably export a larger percentage of its GNP than any other country in the world.

As Japan grows, it will import more manufactured products. Eventually it will probably import more per capita than any other country in the world. The percentage of manufactured products will increase with the amount.

The trading arrangements of Japanese companies for both export and import will increasingly become semipermanent associations, characterized by mutual dependence, rather than arm's-length, spot market arrangements. The Japanese economy must be built on trade, so the trading partner must be equally committed.

Japan is perhaps the most cohesive and culturally integrated of the major industrialized countries in the world. Next to the U.S. and the U.S.S.R., it has the largest population of any industrialized nation. No political combination, such as the Common Market, is likely to achieve both the size and the cultural cohesiveness required to achieve maximum industrial productivity. The U.S.S.R. is, in fact, a diverse collection of cultures within a rather inflexible administrative framework. Japan thus appears to be the nation most likely to equal or surpass the U.S. in standard of living and industrial productivity in this century. If it does so, it will also become the most important factor in international business for American businessmen.

PERPETUATING SUCCESS

All organizations and societies have fringe members who perceive their own interests as outweighing the common interests and who act accordingly. In small numbers, these are the terrorists; in larger numbers, they are the criminal element. In larger aggregations, they are regarded as radical or revolutionary parties.

Increasing general acceptance of the rights of the individual versus the society leads to the toleration of self-serving power groups and eventually to the crumbling of the society into competing power groups who have dissension and cliques within themselves but combine against each other. The process is one of constant combination and alliance for the protection and service of mutual interests and equally constant splitting off of groups and individuals to serve their own interests regardless of the damage that may be inflicted upon the other members of the group, organization or society to which they apparently belong. The balance between these forces establishes the equilibrium which determines the stability of success.

Cooperation and competition must go together for social survival. It is the internal balance between them that determines the viability of society. Cooperation is necessary to achieve productivity. It requires that the individual compromise his own preferences for the benefit of those with whom he must live. Cooperation must provide social benefits. At the same time, competition must eventually eliminate, by Darwinian selection, the influence of those who are least able to contribute to society.

This process of cooperation and competition occurs at several levels:

individual versus individual
group versus group
organization versus organization
nation versus nation
society versus society
culture versus culture

Success in the absence of mutual commitment and identification, and without external threat, leads to the breakdown of cooperation and eventual ineffectiveness. So went many others.

Leadership can perpetuate success and prolong progress by preserving cooperation long after direct external competition fades as a threat. But such leadership succeeds by dramatizing the internal threat of failed cooperation, as well as external competition.

Successful organizations do not explode. They decay and become senile. Their continued success and prosperity depend upon acceptance of values that are the protection against possible future dangers. Continued prosperity is a matter of mutual identification, mutual ideals, and mutual commitment. Success, alone — even overwhelming success — is not enough.

BUSINESS EDUCATION

It is almost certain that the thinking person of 2,000 years ago was as intelligent as today's manager or scientist. Yet all the effort put into building the pyramids could not have placed a human on the moon. People did not know enough.

Because today's accomplishment is built on yesterday's knowledge, this has a profound implication. We cannot surpass the past until we learn its lesson faster than our predecessors. Progress starts only after we have mastered the current state of the art. That is what education is all about. It is the process of compressing the time required to learn that which others have learned before us. If that time can be compressed, then our efforts and energy can be devoted to extending the state of the art, not rediscovering it.

This means that the efficiency of education is a direct determinant of future progress. If it took a lifetime to learn the relevant background, then there would be no time left for extension of that knowledge.

The efficiency of the educational process is a function of many factors, but certainly the means of communicating and storing information is one of its cornerstones. It would have been nearly impossible for the industrial revolution to occur without the printing press being invented at the same time.

The classification, storage, and retrieval of relevant information must be a highly developed art for advanced education to be possible. The day has long passed when an individual could digest, retain, and relate all the information about even a relatively specific field.

The art of teaching has made notable advances in many areas, particularly since learning techniques have focused on relationships and concepts rather than fact accumulation for its own sake. As knowledge increases, it becomes more important to identify that which is relevant, and precisely how and why it is relevant.

This is particularly true of business and business education. Everything is relevant to business. The amount to be known about even a simple business is literally infinite. Yet if this is so, how does a manager know what is important? What is worth remembering? What does the important information signify?

Traditionally, business qualification was based on experience. By acquiring experience and through repetition, it became possible to identify those characteristic factors which were relevant. Yet it is obvious that if experience were the only teacher, then we would on average become as competent as our parents only if our life expectancy exceeded theirs. Significant progress in each generation requires a more efficient teacher than experience.

The foundation of efficient education is the formulation of concepts. This is the skeleton upon which the whole of our body of knowledge must be supported and coordinated. Without concepts to tie facts together, the facts are merely random and often meaningless. Basic concepts make it possible to determine how and where information is relevant.

Therefore, in a very real sense, out ability to become more effective businessmen depends upon our ability to acquire early the key concepts which bring all of our business information into focus.

In the absence of concepts, many business decision-making skills have been intuitive. Often, these intuitive decisions have proven to be almost uncanny in their precision when they were made by experienced and gifted individuals.

Unfortunately, those who are less gifted and less experienced cannot judge the validity of intuitive decisions until long after the fact. Real genius is apt to be unappreciated, particularly if it is ahead of its time. Worst of all, genius is in short supply. In any case, there is little that can be passed intuitively from one management generation to another, even by geniuses.

When our business concepts can be made explicit, then they can be discussed, explored, validated, improved, or taught efficiently. Only when business can be managed in terms of concepts will it be possible to recognize the relative value of the vast amount of data available concerning any business.

Business success will always require finely honed judgment, and theory will always seem a little esoteric. Nevertheless, the future will belong to the businessmen who develop superior concepts, and who explicitly and efficiently pass them on to their associates for improvement.

BUSINESS ETHICS AND SOCIAL RESPONSIBILITY [1]

The social responsibility of business should be clear, explicit, and universally defined by law. Ethics should remain a private and

---

* This is a condensation of a paper prepared for *The Conference on Business Ethics and Social Responsibility* at the University of Virginia, March 28-30, 1974. A more complete version is available on request.

individual matter. The indiscriminate mixing of social preferences, private ethics, and economic interaction is a serious threat to our quality of life.

The role of ethics in business is internal. The members of a business organization should have a common culture, including a common set of values and a common set of expectations. Such values, which are essential to a cooperative endeavor, are enshrined in a code of ethics. The external behavior of the corporation must be consistent with the code of ethics of its staff, since a corporation is its people. But this is the extent to which ethics should affect corporate responsibility.

All business and, indeed, all human relations are based upon certain mutually held assumptions about others' behavior. When these assumptions are invalid or unpredictable, then human cooperation grinds to a halt. Our monetary system built on credit is a simple example. If behavior were unpredictable, then there could be no commerce except face-to-face barter.

Corporations are a creation of the state. They exist only because the state chooses to vest them with the privileges and responsibilities of a real live flesh and blood person. Corporations can sue and be sued, own property, and incur debt. They can act like an individual. This perception of the corporation as a person is misleading if extrapolated to social relationships.

Social responsibility is far down the list of corporate priorities. These priorities are subjective, but they could read something like this:

> Provide customers with lower cost or better service than would otherwise be available. Fail to do this, and there is little justification for existence.
>
> Displace competitors which do not provide as valuable service for the same cost to the customer.
>
> Provide employment that makes use of the abilities of employees more effectively than they could otherwise be used.

Profit is the enabling factor that attracts risk capital and supports debt capability. In the absence of anticipated profit, there is no source of capital except charity or public grants-in-aid. In exactly the same fashion, social responsibility is an incidental and derivative function. In fact, beyond the required, state-specified behavior, social criteria can be counterproductive if it reduces the ability of the corporation to perform its primary functions.

A fundamental conflict exists between the concept of free enterprise and the idea of the corporation as a voluntary contributor to unrelated, nonproductive social benefits. No matter how worthy the cause, a voluntary contribution is a competitive handicap. Free enterprise assumes a competitive system in which all corporate resources are needed to displace the less efficient competition.

Ethics is a private matter. Each person develops his own. However, the need for ethics is a social need produced by the pressure of society. No one can be trusted whose ethics are not known. People must trust each other and be able to predict each other's behavior in order to work together.

Ethics deals with right and wrong, but that does not necessarily mean that a given ethic is right or wrong. Right and wrong are value judgments that vary greatly from culture to culture. Most notions of ethics that are strongly held by large groups of people can properly be called religious beliefs. Most religions profess the belief that they and they alone are right. All others tend to be considered evil or nonhuman, or, at best, dangerously misguided. This ethical self-righteousness is explosive when mixed with others' ethics and an economic system.

The internal culture of an organization can properly be called a code of ethics. This code controls internal status. Violations are severely punished socially. External efforts to change the code will meet with the same passionate defense that religious and political arguments always provoke. At the same time, all organizations, like individuals, adapt over time to their environment in order to survive. To this extent, no business will prosper long which violates the community sense of appropriate behavior. Similarly, change will necessarily be gradual.

The problem does not lie in the ethics-business relationship, but in the potential for polarized, self-contained cultures existing side by side in the same organization or in the same community. Our future will be far brighter if we can encourage more tolerance of divergent views, while simultaneously encouraging thoughtful discussion without polemics.

The real issue is the determination of the relative roles and responsibilities of our institutions. By institutions, I mean all large-scale, formal groups coordinating the use of resources and effort; this includes government, as well as private and public institutions.

Appropriate future roles are questionable for many institutions, including:

large-scale business

government as supplier

private financial institutions

government as banker

professions

private and public universities

legalized monopolies such as labor unions

regulated monopolies

government as regulator

At the heart of the problem is reconciliation of the concept of a market-controlled economy with the popular feeling that any profit is somehow unethical. We must recognize the seriousness of the attack on private enterprise, the market economy, profit as a resource allocator, and large-scale business.

It does not matter that these things are the foundation of our ability to exercise discretion in our style of life. The fact is that the pressures of public opinion are steadily diminishing the ability of private enterprise to make its own decisions in any area. Prices, wages, pensions, information, product design, employment choice, and almost every other decision comes under increasingly detailed regulation. It is not only possible but quite likely that popular feeling will cripple or destroy the whole economic base of our standard of living.

I have a deep-seated fear of large-scale government. I fear its ability to perpetuate itself. I fear the frustration and arrogance inherent in an all-powerful bureaucracy. I fear the degradation of our standard of living. More than all else, I fear the loss of personal freedom as I am regimented, told what to think, how to feel, and what to do.

The characteristics of human behavior have probably changed little throughout recorded history. Ethics has been an ever present issue. As far as business ethics is concerned, I believe the individual business has two responsibilities. First, as an institution, it should live up to the ethics of its own employees. Second, it should, as far as possible, make these ethics into an explicit and common code within the organization. Doesn't every viable institution try to do this?

Ethical leadership in business is internal. If it is well done, the people who make up our large-scale business organizations will demonstrate their leadership among their peers in society.